10-01

D1712478

BRUCE WILLIS

BRUCE WILLIS

Sandy Asirvatham

Introduction by James Scott Brady,
Trustee, the Center to Prevent Handgun Violence
Vice Chairman, the Brain Injury Foundation

Chelsea House Publishers
Philadelphia

Frontispiece: Bruce Willis in the 1995 film Die Hard
with a Vengeance.

CHELSEA HOUSE PUBLISHERS

EDITOR IN CHIEF Sally Cheney
PRODUCTION MANAGER Pamela Loos
ART DIRECTOR Sara Davis
DIRECTOR OF PHOTOGRAPHY Judy L. Hasday
MANAGING EDITOR James D. Gallagher
SENIOR PRODUCTION EDITOR J. Christopher Higgins

Staff for **Bruce Willis**
SENIOR EDITOR LeeAnne Gelletly
EDITORIAL ASSISTANT Robert J. Quinn
ASSOCIATE ART DIRECTOR Takeshi Takahashi
DESIGNER Keith Trego
PICTURE RESEARCHER Patricia Burns
COVER DESIGNER Emiliano Begnardi

The Chelsea House World Wide Web address is:
http://www.chelseahouse.com

First Printing

1 3 5 7 9 8 6 4 2

Library of Congress Cataloging-in-Publication Data

Asirvatham, Sandy.
Bruce Willis / Sandy Asirvatham.
    p.   cm. — (Overcoming adversity)
Includes bibliographical references and index.

ISBN 0-7910-6114-0 (alk. paper) — ISBN 07910-6115-9 (pbk. : alk. paper)

1. Willis, Bruce, 1955—Juvenile literature. 2. Actors—United States—Biography—
Juvenile literature. I. Title. II. Series.
PN2287.W474 A85   2000
791.43'028'092—dc21
[B]   00-045153

CONTENTS

OVERCOMING ADVERSITY

TIM ALLEN
comedian/performer

MAYA ANGELOU
author

THE *APOLLO 13* MISSION
astronauts

LANCE ARMSTRONG
professional cyclist

DREW BARRYMORE
actress

DREW CAREY
comedian/performer

JIM CARREY
comedian/performer

BILL CLINTON
U.S. president

TOM CRUISE
actor

MICHAEL J. FOX
actor

WHOOPI GOLDBERG
comedian/performer

EKATERINA GORDEEVA
figure skater

SCOTT HAMILTON
figure skater

JEWEL
singer and poet

JAMES EARL JONES
actor

QUINCY JONES
musician and producer

ABRAHAM LINCOLN
U.S. president

WILLIAM PENN
Pennsylvania's founder

JACKIE ROBINSON
baseball legend

ROSEANNE
entertainer

MONICA SELES
tennis star

SAMMY SOSA
baseball star

DAVE THOMAS
entrepreneur

SHANIA TWAIN
entertainer

ROBIN WILLIAMS
performer

BRUCE WILLIS
actor

STEVIE WONDER
entertainer

ON FACING ADVERSITY

James Scott Brady

I GUESS IT'S a long way from a Centralia, Illinois, train yard to the George Washington University Hospital Trauma Unit. My dad was a yardmaster for the old Chicago, Burlington & Quincy Railroad. As a child, I used to get to sit in the engineer's lap and imagine what it was like to drive that train. I guess I always have liked being in the "driver's seat."

Years later, however, my interest turned from driving trains to driving campaigns. In 1979, former Texas governor John Connally hired me as a press secretary in his campaign for the American presidency. We lost the Republican primary to a former Hollywood star named Ronald Reagan. But I managed to jump over to the Reagan campaign. When Reagan was elected in 1980, I was "sitting in the catbird seat," as humorist James Thurber would say—poised to be named presidential press secretary. I held that title throughout the eight years of the Reagan administration. But not without one terrible, extended interruption.

It happened barely two months after the Reagan administration took office. I never even heard the shots. On March 30, 1981, my life went blank in an instant. In an attempt to assassinate President Reagan, John Hinckley Jr. armed himself with a "Saturday night special"—a low-quality, $29 pistol—and shot wildly as our presidential entourage exited a Washington hotel. One of the exploding bullets struck me just above the left eye. It shattered into a couple dozen fragments, some of which penetrated my skull and entered my brain.

The next few months of my life were a nightmare of repeated surgery, broken contact with the outside world, and a variety of medical complications. More than once, I was very close to death.

The next few years were filled with frustrating struggles to function with a paralyzed right side, struggles to speak and communicate.

To people who face and defeat daunting obstacles, "ambition" is not becoming wealthy or famous or winning elections or awards. Words like "ambition" and "achievement" and "success" take on very different meanings. The objective is just to live, to wake up every morning. The goals are not lofty; they are very ordinary.

My own heroes are ordinary folks—but they accomplish extraordinary things because they try. My greatest hero is my wife, Sarah. She's accomplished a lot of things in life, but two stand out. The first has been the way she has cared for me and our son since I was shot. A tremendous tragedy and burden was dropped unexpectedly into her life, totally beyond her control and without justification. She could have given up; instead, she focused her energies on preserving our family and returning our lives to normal as much as possible. Week by week, month by month, year by year, she has not reached for the miraculous, just for the normal. Yet in focusing on the normal, she has helped accomplish the miraculous.

Her other most remarkable accomplishment, to me, has been spearheading the effort to keep guns out of the hands of criminals and children in America. Opponents call her a "gun grabber"; I call her a national hero. And I am not alone.

After a seven-year battle, during which Sarah and I worked tirelessly to educate the public about the need for stronger gun laws, the Brady Bill became law in 1993. It was a victory, achieved in the face of tremendous opposition, that now benefits all Americans. From the time the law took effect through fall 1997, background checks had stopped 173,000 criminals and other high-risk purchasers from buying handguns, and the law has helped to reduce illegal gun trafficking.

Sarah was not pursuing fame, or even recognition. She simply started at one point—when our son, Scott, found a loaded handgun on the seat of a pickup truck and, thinking it was a toy, pointed it at Sarah.

Fortunately, no one was hurt. But seeing a gun nearly bring a second tragedy upon our family, Sarah became determined to do whatever she could to prevent senseless death and injury from guns.

Some people think of Sarah as a powerful political force. To me, she's the person who so many times fed me and helped me dress during my long years of recovery.

Overcoming obstacles is part of life, not just for people who are challenged by disabilities, illnesses, or tragedies, but for all people. No matter what the obstacle—fear, disability, prejudice, grief, or a difficulty that isn't likely to "just go away"—we can all work to make this world a better place.

Few would guess Bruce Willis, who first gained fame playing sharp-witted, smooth-talking David Addison in the television series Moonlighting, *struggled for years with a stutter.*

1

LOOK
WHO'S TALKING

WITH A BURST OF FAST, funny, staccato speech, Bruce Willis made his spectacular landing on Planet Television after years of poverty and rejection as a struggling, unknown actor. In 1985, in the pilot episode of the TV show *Moonlighting,* he became David Addison—a wise-cracking, chauvinistic, yet irresistibly charming private detective. Willis delivered his opening bit of dialogue in the pilot program of the show with so much confidence, energy, rhythm, and tunefulness that it sounded like a song:

DAVID ADDISON: *[Standing at his office door and speaking in a rush to his secretary.]*

Now, now, no reason to be shy, let's see a little confidence! A little charisma! A little Dale Carnegie—Remember, Lesson One: Imagine everyone in your audience is completely naked.

[He turns away from the secretary and looks into the eyes of his visitor, the beautiful Maddie Hayes.]

Boggles the mind, doesn't it?

[Under his breath, he turns to the secretary]

Am-scray.

[Then he continues as he leads Maddie into his office.]

Terrible thing, shyness, believe me, I know, but don't
worry, we're going to get her the best help there is,
better than the best! Why, when I first found her, she
was nothing but a poor little urchin out in the street,
an urchin girl, but you don't want to hear that—

MADDIE HAYES: *[She cuts him off with cool sarcasm.]*

I don't want to hear that.

Throughout the two-hour pilot of *Moonlighting* and for
the entire five-year duration of the program, David Addison
talked and talked and talked, interrupted only by Madeline
Hayes's equal volume of fast and furious patter.

This was no small accomplishment for a guy who used
to stutter.

On the show Dave and Maddie, co-owners of the Blue
Moon Detective Agency, were constantly bickering. But
just like the sharp-tongued, sharp-witted couples of the
classic romantic comedies of the 1940s and 1950s, starring screen legends Katharine Hepburn and Spencer Tracy
or Humphrey Bogart and Lauren Bacall, Dave and Maddie
were not-so-secretly in love with each other.

To make the show work, Bruce Willis and his costar,
former model and movie actress Cybill Shepherd, had to
memorize huge chunks of dialogue, then spit them out at
each other with complete clarity, expert comic timing, and
the pace and explosive energy of machine-gun fire. A
show like this required long, hot days of rehearsal and
shooting. The cast was called to the set at six in the morning and did not get to leave until late at night.

Although each episode was packed full of minor characters and guest stars, Willis and Shepherd were in almost
every single scene. Sometimes Willis would start to ad-lib
lines on the set—make them up as he went along.

Although Shepherd was able to respond well with her own improvisations, this spontaneity was a tough challenge for many of the guest stars. On top of all that, Willis and Shepherd started out as total strangers, yet they had to find a way to fill the screen, episode after episode, with the furious friction of a love-hate relationship. Tempers sometimes flared; the angry energy between the fictional characters sometimes spilled over into the real lives of the actors. It was all very hard work.

But the work paid off, in more ways than one. The show became wildly popular all around the world, as television audiences waited anxiously for the day when Dave and Maddie would finally admit their true passion for each other. Because of its stylish dialogue and wicked humor, *Moonlighting* arguably helped raise the standard of excellence for television programs that followed it. The show's producer and writer, a young man named Glenn Gordon Caron, became a powerful person in Hollywood. Cybill Shepherd, whose film career had been going nowhere for years, got the chance to reinvent herself as a true comedic actress, not just another pretty face. And Bruce Willis, who had spent most of the past few years living in a dirty, run-down, one-room apartment and working as a bartender, became a household name almost overnight.

Furthermore, since *Moonlighting* was a show where words counted as much as actions, Willis became not only a famous face, but also one of the world's most forthright, distinctive, and recognizable speaking voices.

Talking had not come easily to this talented young actor. From the age of 8 to 18, Bruce Willis had struggled over nearly every syllable he tried to set free from the awkward prison of his mouth. Yet he had overcome his adolescent stutter and grown into a man who could send words flying out over the airwaves, through the silver screen, and around the world—all the while making it look like the easiest job in the world.

It may seem surprising, but there have been many great

Best known to younger generations for his role in the holiday classic It's a Wonderful Life, *actor Jimmy Stewart (right) became a Hollywood legend despite a childhood stuttering problem.*

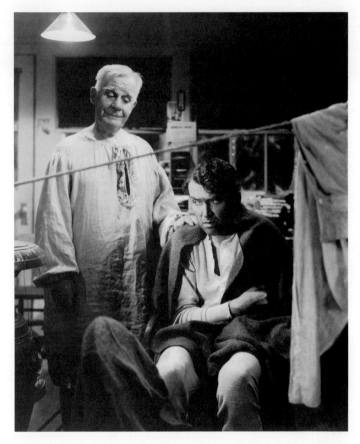

actors and performers who have struggled with speech impediments during childhood and even on through adulthood. Jimmy Stewart (*It's a Wonderful Life,* 1946; *Rear Window,* 1954) and Marilyn Monroe (*Gentlemen Prefer Blondes,* 1953; *Some Like It Hot,* 1959) were two beloved movie stars at the height of Hollywood's "Golden Era." As children, both had stuttered, but they eventually learned to overcome their verbal obstacles and display wit, charm, and eloquence on the big screen. In fact, Monroe developed her unique, breathy, whispering speech style as a way to avoid stuttering.

Today, the main asset of renowned stage and film actor James Earl Jones is his magnificent, rich, deep, rumbling bass voice: he dubbed in the intimidating voice of Darth

Vader in the first three *Star Wars* movies (1977, 1980, and 1983), and he is now best known as a spokesman for Verizon Communications and Cable News Network. But Jones has struggled with a speech impediment all his life. A few years ago he starred in a movie called *A Family Thing* (1996), in which—for the first time ever—he actually used his stutter as part of his portrayal of the character. "I stuttered a bit in the script read-through," Jones said, "and the director thought it would be a good way to show vulnerability in a guy who's a tough cop and a former Marine."

The list of stars who have had to deal with a stutter goes on. Sam Neill, the handsome, brooding Australian actor who starred in *Dead Calm* (1989), *Jurassic Park* (1993), and *The Piano* (1993), is a stutterer. His costar in *The Piano* was Harvey Keitel, yet another actor who stutters. A fixture in early Martin Scorsese gangster movies and a star of Quentin Tarantino's films *Reservoir Dogs* (1992) and *Pulp Fiction* (1994), Keitel is coincidentally also a good friend and former neighbor of Bruce Willis.

Odd as it may seem, some singers also stutter. Legendary country musician Mel Tillis and '70s folk star Carly Simon both struggled with speech impediments while talking. But when singing, they did not have the blocks, repetitions, or long, awkward pauses that stutterers commonly experience.

Stuttering and other speech impediments are not necessarily related to shyness. However, there is a lot of similarity between the child with a speech impediment who talks easily when performing onstage and the shy child who miraculously becomes a chatterbox and exhibitionist when acting in the lead role of the school play. What explains the mysterious transformation in verbal ability that occurs when they play to an audience?

The first thing to understand is that no one knows for certain what causes a person to stutter. It was once believed to be a form of mental illness, an ailment that was strictly related to the mind. As to the root cause of stuttering, the theories ranged from childhood trauma to bad mothering. Newer research seems to point in the opposite direction, to problems or abnormalities that are physical in nature—or more specifically, neurological (that is, of or relating to the body's nervous system: the brain, spinal cord, and nerves).

In tests that compared the brain chemistry and neuro-electrical impulses of stutterers and nonstutterers, investigators found some differences. (Incidentally, there is no perfect or absolute distinction between these two classes of speakers: all individuals are subject to verbal blocks or hesitations, especially under conditions of exhaustion or stress. But stutterers stumble upon these communication obstacles much more frequently or more severely than most people.) The latest research suggests that stuttering is associated with dopamine, a neurochemical that occurs naturally in the brain. In stutterers, abnormally high levels of dopamine have been found in the part of the brain that controls speech.

But although stuttering may be related physically to the brain's function, there is still a proverbial "chicken and egg" question that needs answering: Which came first? In other words, it's not clear whether the stuttering is caused by, or is the cause of, the difference in brain activity patterns. What is clear from the evidence is that psychological factors (such as behavioral or mental characteristics) also play a large part in the ailment—perhaps in its onset, and also in its possible remedies.

That's because the fear of stuttering itself leads to more stuttering. There's a two-way relationship between mind and body, a kind of feedback loop that operates between the physical aspects and the psychological aspects of all ailments, including speech difficulties. Whether the ultimate cause is psychological trauma or physical defect, the effect is that *something* is going wrong in the person's neurological speech center—the part of the brain controlling expression of one's thoughts. The flaw makes the stutterer unable to say what he or she wants to say, which makes the person nervous, angry, and frustrated, which causes various electrical and chemical signals in his or her brain to go haywire, which causes the whole vicious cycle to repeat itself.

There can be a deep shame associated with being unable to express one's thoughts. Bruce Willis once described his schoolboy predicament: "I could hardly talk. It took me three minutes to complete a sentence. It was crushing for anyone who wanted to express themselves, who wanted to be heard and couldn't. It was frightening."

James Earl Jones once described stuttering as "one of the most agonizing things for a child. And it usually surfaces just at the point when they're trying to express themselves." Jones recalled stumbling over words during childhood Bible classes back in his hometown of Arkabutla, Mississippi: "I'd say something, and the other kids would laugh."

So why is it that, for some people, pretending to be someone else helps break that feedback loop of stuttering—shame—more stuttering? John C. Harrison, program director of the National Stuttering Project, who was himself a stutterer, has a plausible theory having to do with self-image and self-esteem. Stutterers, he believes, are often naturally stronger personalities than their poor self-image will allow them to show. Secretly they are "more opinionated, more emotional, more excited, . . . more responsible, more authoritative" than they let other people know. But after years of being ridiculed for their lack of verbal fluency, they've developed a shell and a habit of not bothering to express themselves, since it hardly seems worth all the trouble.

"We took our excitement and natural enthusiasm and aliveness—our *real self*—and learned how to block it out

In the 1996 film A Family Thing, *actor James Earl Jones portrays a character with a stutter—the same disability he overcame as a child. Today, the former stutterer is known as the voice of the Cable News Network and Verizon Communications.*

so no one, not even we, could see it," Harrison says. In pretending to be someone else, stutterers may find that all their hidden personality traits come tumbling out of them in big, complete sentences, long before they fall into a spiral of self-doubt, long before their brain chemistry even has a chance to go haywire.

Harrison's theory sounds a lot like what Bruce Willis believes about his own boyhood struggles. In an interview with *Playboy* magazine Bruce explained, "[My stuttering] was based on psychological things, on fears, on self-worth, on how I viewed myself. It came out of a fear of not being good enough, of having something wrong with me. Just fear of the world, of my place in the world."

Singer Carly Simon is also someone who believes her problem was brought on by emotional factors. She started stuttering severely when she was eight years old and became aware of her mother's extramarital affair, which caused an atmosphere of jealousy, anger, lies, and deception within the Simon household. After undergoing therapy with a psychiatrist, who unsuccessfully tried to help Carly stop stuttering, she turned to singing and songwriting. "I felt so strangulated talking that I did the natural thing," she explained, "which is to write songs." Like many stutterers, Simon found singing trouble-free in comparison to speaking. This may be because the processes that control singing and speaking take place in two separate areas of the brain.

In most cases, stuttering is thought to be caused by a combination of two factors: "nature" (the physical features of your body and brain) and "nurture" (the environmental influences around you, such as the kind of family relationships you have). It's possible that some people have a potential to become stutterers but that this potential develops only under stress, such as the stress that Carly Simon felt in her household environment.

These days there are almost as many different proposed "cures" and therapies for stuttering as there are people who stutter. One common treatment, though, is relaxation

therapy. It was a college speech therapist who taught Bruce Willis certain muscular relaxation techniques to loosen up his whole body, including his jaw and tongue. Other treatments for stuttering have involved the use of drugs. Long before people understood the health dangers of using cigarettes, Charles Lamb, an early-19th-century English essayist who stuttered, proposed smoking large quantities of tobacco as one way to relax the tongue.

Today researchers are experimenting with some new medications that correct the dopamine imbalance seen in people who stutter. Drugs that reduce the level of dopamine in the brain, called dopamine inhibitors, have successfully reduced the frequency of stuttering by about 50 percent in subjects tested.

Interestingly, there is also a growing self-acceptance

A four-year-old boy works with his speech therapist. Although no one really knows what causes stuttering, certain techniques can make speaking easier for the stutterer. These include repeating phrases, singing, and lowering the pitch of one's voice.

Like Bruce Willis, Carly Simon found that performing helped her overcome her stutter. In her case it was singing instead of acting that served as the best therapy.

movement among stutterers, who want to be treated with respect by other people, whether or not they choose to try to stop stuttering. As Mel Tillis explains, he chose to accept his disability when he was a young man just starting to have success as a country singer in the late 1950s: "I told myself that if I couldn't quit stuttering, then the world was going to have to take me like I was. What you see is what you get." Although he has never overcome his stuttering, his brash attitude has helped him stay focused on the things that are important to him: singing and performing and telling jokes onstage—even jokes in which he makes fun of his own speech troubles. And that brazen attitude helped him secure such successes as winning the 1976 Country Music Entertainer of the Year Award.

In the end, it's clear that each individual case is unique. In Willis's particular situation something about being an actor—about pretending to be someone he wasn't—helped him overcome his speech difficulties. He no longer stutters, even when being himself. Or, at the very least, he no longer stutters when he's being "Bruce Willis," a public figure who has to express himself to directors, other actors, and TV and magazine reporters as part of his job. Only his loved ones and closest friends would know whether the private Bruce Willis still has trouble with words. Nevertheless, stuttering would be just one of many obstacles that Bruce Willis would overcome on his path to becoming a star.

Active in the student government and drama club, Bruce (right) became a popular guy at Penns Grove High School, where he used humor as a way to compensate for his stutter.

2

LAST MAN STANDING

BRUCE WILLIS WAS always destined to be "one of the guys"—loud, funny, argumentative, boisterous, and arrogant. In the male-dominated, blue-collar environment of Willis's adolescence and young adulthood, this was simply the way men were expected to behave—to be the tough guy, the last man standing in a fight. In the 1960s and 1970s, in factory towns all over the United States, lots of boys were growing up to be joke-telling, bar-brawling tough guys, just like Willis and his friends. What's unusual is the way Willis was able to take this background and transform it into the gritty but charming TV and movie characters that ultimately captivated audiences around the world.

Willis has never been shy about discussing his humble roots. As he once told a reporter, he came from a "long line of welders and mechanics," skilled blue-collar workers with little formal education and not much hope of moving up in the world. His father, David Willis, was an army engineer. In the early 1950s, David Willis was stationed in Germany, where, like many of his fellow servicemen, he dated a local girl. Nineteen-year-old Marlene spoke very little English, and there's a good

Parents Marlene and David Willis divorced when Bruce was just 16 years old. Deeply affected by the divorce, he later noted that the lack of affection in his home may have contributed to his early speech disability.

chance her romance with the young American soldier would have ended as soon as David received his next army assignment in a new town or country. Instead, Marlene got pregnant. David did what was considered the honorable thing and married Marlene.

On March 19, 1955, shortly after the wedding, the child was born in his mother's hometown of Idar-Oberstein, West Germany, and was christened Walter Bruce Willis. When the boy was two years old, David Willis moved his family back to his hometown of Carneys Point in southern

New Jersey, near the Delaware River. Years later the actor would remember his hometown as a "cool place to grow up": a split-personality town nestled between the big, grimy factories and busy waterfront piers near the river and the quiet, green farmland and open countryside to the south and east.

In the mid-1950s, when Walter Bruce Willis was still a young child, much of American popular culture—particularly Hollywood—was emphasizing the idea of manhood. Sometimes this focus was a celebration of men's strength and bravery, as in *On the Waterfront* (1954). In this classic movie Marlon Brando portrays a dockworker and former boxer, a role for which he won an Oscar. Brando's character, Terry Malloy, is a brooding, violent man who manages to become heroic through his honesty and integrity. At other times, though, Hollywood took a more critical view of the young American male. In *Rebel Without a Cause* (1955), James Dean plays a teenage hooligan who is alienated from his family and friends; filled with angry, destructive energy, he has no real ideals or creative goals in life.

If Willis hadn't found his way into acting and performing, his life might have turned out looking very much like a James Dean movie. Although his father's side of the family (his father, grandfather, and uncles) was fairly close-knit, there wasn't much happiness or emotional closeness within his immediate family (his mother and father, who were having marital problems, and his three younger siblings—Florence, Robert, and David).

This unhappy home life made Walter Bruce Willis insecure as a young boy and may have contributed to the onset of his stuttering when he was eight years old. He became shy and withdrawn, as his speech impediment caused him to stumble over words and struggle to complete a sentence. As one of his school friends, Bruce Alissi, later remembered, Willis was "a scared little guy who hardly ever talked for fear of being teased. He just kept out of the way, back of the class, never getting involved unless he had to."

But by his early teenage years Willis began to make changes. He dropped his first name in preference for his middle name, calling himself Bruce. And he started to overcompensate for his natural shyness and insecurity by becoming the class clown and prankster. It could be said that these were his earliest experiments with "performing." Years later one of Willis's teachers at Penns Grove High School, Anthony Rastelli, described his former student for

When Bruce Willis was growing up, the popular culture glorified actors such as Marlon Brando, who played nonconforming, sometimes violent, characters such as Terry Malloy in the Oscar-winning film On the Waterfront. *Bruce would one day present a similar "tough guy" image.*

biographer John Parker. Rastelli recalled how Bruce began to overcome his stuttering disability as he gradually moved from the back of the class to center of attention:

> At that age where boys begin to find their feet, Willis had a hard time. The stammer was a problem and in the end, he began to compensate for it by his antics. He had to establish himself among the pack, and unable to do so with fluent speech, he did it another way—making himself stand out in the crowd by becoming the joker, the

mini-tearaway. What he was doing was saying, 'Yes, I stutter—but that doesn't mean I'm not as good as the rest of you, better even.' He made the others like him—and they did, although you could never eliminate the cruelty that exists when youngsters have someone in the midst who is afflicted by impediment or some other setback.

Rastelli goes on to describe young Bruce's first difficult attempts at speaking in front of an audience. "I nearly died for him when he went on stage to make a speech. The kids were all laughing but somehow, he stuck it out and finished his piece, which was fairly typical of his spirit. And eventually, of course, he discovered that in front of an audience, he could overcome his disability."

Willis once told an interviewer, "A big part of my sense of humor came out of my stuttering, in trying to overcome that and have some dignity. I said, 'Yes, I stutter, but I can make you laugh.'" Dignity, however, clearly wasn't always the top priority. As one of his pranks as a teenager, Willis showed up at a fancy school dress party wearing nothing but a baby diaper. It was a freezing cold night, but Bruce didn't care, his friends remembered, as long as he got his laughs. Another time Bruce stripped naked except for a pair of sneakers and some sunglasses and went streaking through the center of town.

Not surprisingly, though, the young rabble-rouser still had a quiet, private, self-motivated side to his personality. Although Bruce was mostly a C student, he started to become an avid reader, and to this day he says reading is one of the great joys in his life. As he recalled years later, the first book that really hooked him on reading was a seventh grade text on mythology. "And then I read *Great Expectations* in a week," he noted. "I was mesmerized by Dickens." He read J. R. R. Tolkien's *Lord of the Rings* trilogy "at least 15 times," praising the series for its rich detail and heroic qualities. "I can open those books now at any place and know right where I am." Later on he became enamored of more contemporary writers, including Elmore Leonard, T. Coraghessan Boyle, John Irving, Arthur C. Clarke, and Larry McMurtry. He read Ken Kesey's classic *One Flew over the Cuckoo's Nest* five times. And although the works of William Shakespeare were difficult for him at first, he continued to work at reading the Bard's plays and sonnets on into adulthood, as he explained, "just to hear myself say a different language."

Willis also fell in love with music, particularly soul and rhythm-and-blues (R&B), the sounds coming from the African-American musicians of Philadelphia and Detroit. He loved blues guitarists and vocalists like Muddy Waters, John Lee Hooker, and "Mississippi" Fred McDowell. In his youth he also listened to the rock artists Mott the Hoople, the Rolling Stones, Led Zeppelin, and Jimi Hendrix.

Bruce taught himself to sing the blues and play the harmonica. He even bought a used saxophone and tried to become proficient. Because the Willis family was living in a small apartment at the time, Bruce would sometimes go far out in the backyard and play his sax, so as not to drive his parents and siblings crazy.

The Willises' marriage had never been a strong one, and just after Bruce's 16th birthday David and Marlene divorced. Bruce chose to live with his father, while his two brothers and one sister stayed with his mother. "It was a rending, tearing thing," he later remembered.

Although the divorce affected the family very deeply, Bruce continued to emerge from his shell and sought more and more ways to attract attention to himself. Realizing that his stutter vanished whenever he played a character onstage, he joined the drama club and took small roles in many school productions.

With his popularity and sense of humor, Bruce easily won the election for president of the student council in his senior year. That same year, he was accused of helping start a fight between black kids and white kids in the school cafeteria. Although this was one of many "race

riots" that took place in the school during Willis's time
there, he later came to believe that these incidents were not
really about race relations. Instead, he said, they were
about "17- and 18-year-olds needing to fight."

In any case, more than a hundred boys were involved in
this particular incident. And Bruce was identified as one of
the instigators of the conflict, a charge he flatly denied. In
fact, Willis and his friends insisted they had been trying to
calm the rioters, not inflame them further. After an official
investigation and a two-month suspension, the school
withdrew the charges against Bruce and reversed its decision to expel him. His high school graduation came and
went with no further fireworks.

Years later these childhood experiences would filter into
the way Willis carried himself onstage and on-screen.
Although he left high school with no clear ambition to
become an actor, his early "training" had already begun: he
was teaching himself to be the tough, funny, charming, but
also deeply private man he'd eventually portray in movies.

The tough-guy vision of American manhood was still
the norm in popular culture when Willis was growing up
in the 1960s and 1970s. But by the time he actually started
to pursue acting seriously in the late 1970s and early
1980s, circumstances had changed. For one thing, the
women's movement had created new images of female
strength, independence, and assertiveness. In some cases
certain men found their previous dominant roles being
challenged, diminished, or eliminated altogether under
new feminist ways of thinking and behaving. Television
and movies had begun to reflect this, at least in some small
ways. Women characters became more demanding and
articulate, and men were expected to respond more sensi-
tively to their demands.

The "new man" wasn't a ruffian like James Dean or a
mumbling, brooding, muscle-bound hero like Marlon
Brando. Instead, he was a witty but nonthreatening guy
like Alan Alda, star of the hit TV show *M*A*S*H,* or

filmmaker/actor Woody Allen, who still expressed love and desire for beautiful women, but was more of a talker and thinker than a man of action.

Back in Carneys Point, however, men in real life still tended to behave more like the blue-collar heroes of the previous era: working hard all week long at backbreaking factory jobs, spending Friday nights drinking and laughing in the company of their male friends, chasing after women but not getting involved in serious relationships, occasionally getting into fistfights. This was what it meant to be one of the guys, and Willis was no exception.

After graduating from Penns Grove High School, Bruce took a job working at a DuPont factory in Deepwater, New Jersey. Several low-paying jobs later, he finally realized he wanted more out of life, and enrolled at Montclair State College.

3

NOBODY'S FOOL

BRUCE WILLIS LEFT high school with no real plans, no real vision of what his life was about. For a boy from the working-class world of southern New Jersey, the idea of actually pursuing an acting career would have been a far-off, crazy dream. In fact, Willis reached young adulthood without any idea of his goals whatsoever, whether in acting or other pursuits.

Years later Bruce would tell an interviewer that the only things he'd learned in high school were how to be a troublemaker and how to "beat the system," as he put it. "High school helped my acting a great deal, because it taught me how to lie with a straight face. I'd cut class and go back and get snagged by the assistant principal, and he'd look right at me and I'd say, 'Just went out to my car to get a book.'"

But Bruce also complained about what he didn't learn in high school: "[It] didn't teach me . . . common sense. It didn't teach me communication skills. How to deal with conflict. How to balance my checkbook. It didn't teach me anything about life." In that uninspiring environment, without any alternative guidance or role models, he had little choice but to follow in his father's footsteps.

A few years earlier that would have meant working in the family machine shop. Bruce explained, "I come from a long line of blue-collar people: My grandfather, my father and all my uncles owned a machine shop that I grew up around. When I was 13, I started working there in the summertime. I learned how to repair small engines. When I was 14, I knew how to weld."

But by the time Bruce graduated from high school, David Willis had sold the family business and given up his attempts to succeed as a self-employed welder. Now he was working at the DuPont chemical factory in a neighboring town called Deepwater, New Jersey. Bruce got a dull but steady-paying position there driving a truck that shuttled factory workers from one side of the large plant to the other. He hated the job. A few months after he was hired, Willis witnessed a terrible accident: "A guy got blown up. I was about a mile away, and I saw the explosion. It was a big drum, about the size of a house, in which they mixed chemicals. This guy happened to be driving a truck past the building, which I also drove by ten times a day."

A few days after the fatal accident, Bruce quit his job. He later claimed that he personally wasn't that deeply affected by the incident: "What made me think about quitting was the way the other guys, the older ones who had been there for ten or twenty years, took it. They were gone; just white. That's me in twenty years' time? No way. I left at the end of the week."

Bruce's decision to quit his factory job was just the first of many rash, impulsive moves he would make over the next few years. Clearly, he had always had a restlessness inside him, an impatience with the status quo, and a willingness to take risks. He didn't know what he was looking for yet, but he knew he was looking for something better than what his background promised.

Willis's second job was almost as dull as the first one, and maybe even a little more dangerous. For $2.80 an hour, he worked as a night security guard at the construction site of a nuclear power plant in Penns Grove, New Jersey. The job responsibilities, as he explained, were fairly simple: "I was walking outdoors in the snow with these keys, making sure that [the power plant] was safe. It was a pretty weird environment. I used to go 300 feet underground to a nuclear container to hit these keys that punched a time clock. It was very spooky."

The one advantage of Bruce's job was that he could practice his harmonica while making his rounds. In the quiet of the nuclear container, 300 feet underground, Willis found that his harmonica sounded great. It sounded even better when he blasted his music over the company's public announcement system. According to Willis's biographer John Parker, "there are plenty of workers in Penns Grove today who remember being ear-blasted by the youth who became Bruce Willis."

Very soon Willis jumped out of this job in his usual impulsive manner and spent a few months doing nothing but tending bar, playing in a local blues band, and hanging around with his friends. True, he was still a voracious reader, and was starting to vaguely think about going back to school and getting the education he'd mostly missed while skipping classes and playing all those pranks in high school. But today, as a middle-aged man, he might still be doing a lot of the same things—working at mind-numbing jobs, living paycheck to paycheck, getting drunk and rowdy, dreaming impractical dreams—if he hadn't run into his high school Latin teacher, Grace Dilks.

Dilks had always believed in Bruce's potential as an actor, even though his speech impediment still created a problem for him. When she saw Willis again after graduation, she was more than merely encouraging—she pushed him to enroll at Montclair State College, up in the northeastern part of New Jersey. It was an inexpensive school for state residents, and it boasted an excellent performing arts department. Grace Dilks was so enthusiastic about

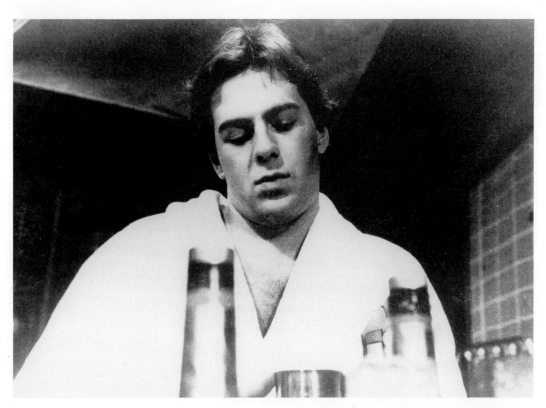

Bruce's tendency to stutter disappeared onstage—whether he was playing Brick in Tennessee Williams's Cat on a Hot Tin Roof *(above) or performing in Jean-Baptiste Moliére's* The Miser *(facing page, center). While at Montclair State, Willis discovered acting as a potential career.*

Willis's future that she even offered to drive him to the enrollment office.

It was the era of gas rationing, right after the Middle East oil crisis of 1973–74. Even though Dilks knew she might not have enough gas to get to Montclair State and back, she took Willis anyway. "It was like driving into the desert without water," she recalled later. "I knew we were going to run out of gas and sure enough, we did on the way back. Bruce kept up a running banter while we waited for the state troopers who carried emergency supplies."

According to Bruce, the stutter began to fade when he started to take more responsibility and stand on his own two feet. It was also during his first year at Montclair State that Willis truly got his speech impediment under control with the help of a therapist. As Bruce explains, the speech therapist's method consisted largely of relaxation

exercises: "He would make me start with my toes and relax every joint and muscle in my body and then have me talk." In that state of mind and body, Willis noted, "it was impossible to stutter."

Incidentally, Bruce was one of the lucky ones for whom speech therapy actually worked. Unfortunately, many other people with speech impediments suffer a frustrating pattern: they easily become fluent within the protected walls of the therapist's office but then start stuttering again as soon as they try to express themselves in public.

Along with formal therapy Willis received a kind of unofficial "treatment" every time he walked on the Montclair State stage to rehearse or perform a dramatic role. As he later described his experiences onstage, "[W]henever I acted, I didn't stutter." In pretending to be somebody else,

Willis was somehow able to relax completely.

Bruce was not an instant star or a brilliant natural actor. His first major role was the young man named Brick in the play by Tennessee Williams, *Cat on a Hot Tin Roof*—this was the same character that one of his personal heroes, actor Paul Newman, had played in the 1958 movie version. Willis's performances in this play and other Montclair State productions were considered competent, but not highly noteworthy. And yet he always exhibited that impatience, that restless quality, that well-developed sense of humor, and that ability to bluff—strong qualities that came through on the stage as well as in real life.

Still, Bruce's teachers at Montclair State considered it the height of arrogance and foolishness when, after only 18 months, he decided to quit college. In his teachers' minds this impatient, overly confident youngster still needed a lot more training and experience before trying his hand at professional auditions for Off-Broadway productions. But in Bruce's mind he was ready.

In late 1976, Willis got lucky and landed a job in New York, as an assistant stage manager understudying the lead role in a tiny, obscure, Off-Off-Broadway play called *Heaven and Earth*. Unfortunately, the play had a limited run and didn't pay very well.

But then in early 1977, a dire family situation forced Willis into a temporary retreat: he moved out of Manhattan and back to Carneys Point to help care for his 19-year-old sister, Florence, who'd been diagnosed with a deadly form of cancer, and for one of his brothers, who'd been injured in a car accident. Penniless and impatient, but loyal to his family, Bruce stayed for about five months. Then his sister made him promise that he'd return to New York and become a star. In a few years Florence Willis would fully recover from her cancer, but at the time there wasn't a lot of hope for her. So Bruce was moved by what seemed to be one of his sister's last wishes on this earth. He worked for a few months at a local health club, scraped together a little money, and returned to the Big Apple for his second foray into the theatrical world.

As David Willis said years later, "[Bruce was] determined to make it. Personally, I wasn't that optimistic. But I thought he had to get it out of his system."

As Bruno the bartender, aspiring actor Bruce Willis entered the New York City scene. With his sharp wit and easygoing personality, he quickly made friends with the customers, some of whom would later provide leads for his acting career.

4

THE RETURN
OF BRUNO

AS A BOY, WILLIS had gone by the nickname Bruno. Maybe it was a pet name given him by his parents, or maybe it was a new label he'd chosen for himself in trying to escape his shy, stutterer's persona and reinvent himself as the class clown. But in any case, it was a moniker that seemed to suggest a certain very specific kind of young man: a fun-loving guy, loyal and easygoing, but also the kind of guy who wouldn't hesitate to give you a good thrashing if you provoked him.

If you were a screenwriter working on, let's say, a film about gangsters set in 1920s Chicago, or jazz musicians in New York's Greenwich Village in the 1960s, or gold prospectors in San Francisco in the mid-19th century, Bruno might be the name you'd choose for the bartender character; he is a man who simultaneously pours mixed drinks, tells jokes to his male customers, flirts with his female customers, and keeps one watchful eye out for potential troublemakers. Bruno is the name of a guy who can hobnob easily with powerful and famous people but who never mistreats his less well-heeled patrons. Bruno is the name of a guy with dozens upon dozens of people he calls friends.

In 1977, Bruce Willis left Carneys Point. He signed his name on the lease for a tiny, dimly lit railroad-style apartment that essentially consisted of one long, narrow room on the fifth floor of a building with no elevator. Located in the cheap but sleazy midtown Manhattan neighborhood of Hell's Kitchen, the apartment was close to the Broadway theater district. Soon after moving in, Willis began living life as "Bruno"—actor, bartender, and all-around good-time guy.

Bruce quickly found work at a busy, trendy uptown bar called Café Central, where he befriended a lot of people in show business, some of them struggling unknowns such as himself, some of them bona fide stars. The bar scene attracted "a mishmash of models and actors and wannabes," as another customer later described it. Among Bruce's friends and acquaintances were famous singers such as Cher, James Taylor, and Sting (who was then leader of the innovative reggae rock band the Police), along with up-and-coming actors such as Robert Duvall, Richard Gere, Mickey Rourke, Peter Weller, and Treat Williams.

Even among these professional performers, Willis was still the "class clown" and the natural center of attention. He'd tell jokes, zip around the bar with a smirk on his face, or even jump straight over the bar to deal handily with any drunken troublemakers. Sometimes, late at night, he'd pull out his harmonica to accompany James Taylor's guitar playing. As Café Central's owner, Larry McIntyre, remembered years later, Willis had "class" in his manner, but was also "very entertaining, very funny and acerbically witty, which the customers enjoyed." A friend from that time, Joey Plewa, recalled the New York Bruno days: "If there was anybody who knew how to have fun, it was Bruce. He exuded an electric feeling, wanting everybody around him to have fun."

As novelist and magazine writer Jay McInerney pointed out in a 1995 *Esquire* profile of the famous actor, "Bruno" Willis also belonged to the informal "fraternity of guys who tended bar on the Upper West Side in the early eight-ies"—a group very reminiscent of the factory gang he'd left behind in small-town New Jersey. Many of these men would remain friends with Willis even after he became a star. One of Willis's buddies, who later became a music-video producer, described the camaraderie as "an Oakland Raider kind of thing—once you're on the team, you're never off the team."

But while Bruce was an instant and smashing success within the social realm of New York's trendy bars and cafés, he was not climbing the ladder very quickly as an aspiring professional actor. True, his barroom network of friends were sometimes helpful in his search for acting work. Treat Williams tipped Willis off about the auditions for supporting roles in the Paul Newman movie *The Verdict* (1982). Willis received a bit part in the film as a news reporter—a role so small that his name didn't even appear in the credits. This easily overlooked performance was, needless to say, not followed by any new offers for a starring film role or any calls from agents begging to rep-resent Willis on his imminent climb to the top.

Still, Bruno maintained his ambition and optimism. He'd left behind the uninspiring muddle of his Carneys Point youth and was now focused on his goals. He took as much work as he could get in Off-Broadway productions and TV commercials—most notably, several spots for Levi's 501 blue jeans—and supported himself in between with bartender jobs. As he told *Rolling Stone* magazine years later, he was always quite confident in his approach: "[Y]ou can either go to New York and learn your craft . . . or you can go right to Hollywood and try to break into TV with your looks or charm or personal style, whatever it is people do. And I think I did the right thing, went to New York and got most of my experience from working, onstage and Off-Broadway, not for money, just working in front of a house [a live theater audience]."

It was around this time that Willis met Sheri Rivera,

Although his first big break in film was an uncredited role in The Verdict, *Bruce had the chance to work with Paul Newman—an actor he had admired since childhood.*

ex-wife of the controversial TV reporter and future talk-show host Geraldo Rivera. Sheri was an aspiring writer with plenty of friends and show-business acquaintances in Manhattan. She became Willis's first serious girlfriend and a major influence on the development of his career.

Looking back on the early days of his acting career, Willis would count his appearance in the Off-Broadway production of Sam Shepard's play *Fool for Love* as his first truly lucky break. In 1984, Will Patton, an established actor who had the lead role of Eddie in this long-running play, went to the bar where Bruce was working and told him he was going to quit. With this knowledge the brash Willis showed up at the theater and demanded to audition for the role. This was the kind of thing he'd always do—show up unannounced for every audition he could get to, even closed or private casting calls, and demand to be given a chance. Because he'd been coached by Will Patton, Bruce knew exactly how to approach his reading for the role, and he got the job.

Still the ever-popular "class president" in some ways, Willis was able to fill the small theater with his friends and cronies from all his bar gigs and previous acting jobs. They may have all been enticed to show up simply for the pleasure of seeing their friend Bruno on the stage—but many of them left the play impressed with Bruce's work.

Sixteen years later *New York Times* film critic Elvis Mitchell would remember young Bruce Willis's appearance in this tense, disturbing, controversial play. Mitchell recalled that Willis's natural "capacity for ache was the core of his performance onstage. . . . His face was closed off, and his presence was riveting. He wasn't quite able to use his voice onstage [in an effectively dramatic manner, but] he got by on ambition and the energy expended for a live audience." Willis would tell *Rolling Stone* magazine that the role of Eddie was a deeply important step in his development as an actor: "I miss Eddie so much. It was a ninety-minute one-act, and the preparation was so intense it just transformed me."

As always, it helped Bruce to have friends in relatively high places. Sheri Rivera—who was, in many ways, just as bold and aggressive a personality as her boyfriend—managed to drag a well-established actor's agent, Gene Parseghian, to the show, even though Parseghian complained that he had a general policy against seeing unknown replacement actors in small Off-Broadway productions. But after seeing Bruce's performance, Parseghian was impressed enough to take the aspiring actor on as a client at his agency, Triad Theatrical.

Now that Willis had an agent, it seemed things were finally going to start happening for him. Within a month Triad had booked Bruce for a screen test (an audition) for the film *Desperately Seeking Susan,* which would star pop singer Madonna and actress Rosanna Arquette. Willis was auditioning for the part of a punk-rock musician

Bruce's girlfriend Sheri Rivera,
who had many show-business
contacts, was an influential
force on his early career.

(Madonna's love interest in the film), and his agent
required him to dress the part. Accordingly, Bruce arrived
at the screen test wearing fake tattoos, earrings, and a
rough, uneven haircut—but he didn't get the job. The role
went instead to Aidan Quinn, who was then almost as
unknown as Willis.

Down to his last dollars but energized by Sheri's optimism and his new agent's encouragement, Willis decided

to take his first trip to Hollywood, just to catch some of the events at the 1984 Summer Olympics in Los Angeles and to casually check out potential acting opportunities. Bruce wasn't expecting a lot; in fact, he was still sporting the punk-rock look he'd adopted for the Madonna movie audition—an overall image that would probably disqualify him on the spot from most casting calls.

Willis was still bartending in New York, though he now worked at the Kamikaze Bar, run by a former coworker at Café Central. Biographer John Parker describes an encounter between Willis and his boss that took place just days before the Hollywood trip:

> Before [Willis] left, he called in on Kirke Walsh at the Kamikaze. There was more than a touch of apprehension about him. The bravado facade had once again melted.
>
> "I'll be broke when I get back," Willis told him.
>
> "No problem," said Walsh. "Your job will still be open." Willis took a slug at his beer bottle, and pondered for a moment.
>
> "I don't think I want to work the bar anymore."
> "Okay," said Walsh. "But I was thinking about making you manager."
>
> Willis pulled out his harmonica and blew some bluesy notes, then dashed off into the night.

In a role that almost didn't make it to television, Bruce Willis found himself within striking distance of Hollywood stardom with his portrayal of Moonlighting's *David Addison. He's seen here just after receiving the 1987 Emmy for Outstanding Lead Actor in a Drama Series.*

5

STRIKING DISTANCE

WRITER/PRODUCER Glenn Gordon Caron and his coproducers had auditioned 3,000 men in 10 cities in their search for the right fit for the character of David Addison, the leading man for the new TV show *Moonlighting.* So far, it had been a fruitless search. The producers had already secured Cybill Shepherd for the female lead, offering to pay her $50,000 an episode (a huge TV salary in those days). But the ABC network was ready to pull the plug on the project if Caron couldn't find the right leading man. Caron explained later, "I wanted a guy who plants his feet and speaks his mind and deals with women as he deals with men."

Timing is everything. One day during his California visit Willis dropped by the Los Angeles office of his agency, Triad Theatrical. There an agent named Jenny Delaney took one look at Willis—still displaying his punk-rock persona: army fatigues, beat-up khaki shirt, earrings, unevenly cropped hair sticking up all over the place—and picked up the phone to call the *Moonlighting* executives.

"Bruce was not expecting to be sent out to an audition," Delaney later remembered. "He basically just wandered in off the street."

Willis was given a few pages of the script to prepare for the audition. He sat in a bar reading the script and laughing. The material was verbose and witty, and Willis felt confident he could nail the part. On the day Caron and the ABC executives were looking at their final 15 candidates, Willis showed up.

"There's an etiquette that happens at auditions," Willis explained later. "You walk in, and especially if you want the job, you're very polite." But Willis was feeling cavalier, in part because he really didn't believe he'd get the role, so he felt no real pressure. He strutted in and said, "Hi, how are you, I'm Bruce Willis, let's do it."

As Bruce later recalled, "I knew I could do this man's material; I recognized an offbeat character, a guy on the edge who's horsing around out there where the air's real thin. I just did the thing, this rocking scene that's in the pilot, just burned it and said, 'Thanks, see ya,' and walked out."

Although the other ABC executives were unimpressed, Caron was instantly convinced he'd finally found his David Addison. Not just that: he was convinced he'd discovered a future superstar. In an article published later in the *Los Angeles Times,* Caron recalled his initial reaction to Willis's performance. At that time he was living in a place called Hidden Hills, he explained, about an hour's drive from the production studios: "We would work a 14- or 15-hour day, and I was always concerned I was going to die making the trip home because I was so tired. But I remember the day I found Bruce, I thought, 'It's OK, because if I die they have got to give my wife a million bucks because I have found a whole new guy.'" Caron made an accurate prophecy that day. Not only was Bruce Willis right for the part of David Addison; Bruce Willis was "a whole new industry."

Caron said Willis's screen test was not a perfect reading of the character—it was an "aggressive and not terribly funny performance." But he could see that Willis

understood the material. "And the force of his personality, for me anyway, was something to behold. . . . You'd be walking down the aisle with him and all the secretaries would be abuzz."

Willis certainly didn't fit the image of the clean-cut, classically good-looking leading men of the mid-1980s TV shows and movies, so Caron had to work hard to persuade ABC executives to give Bruce the role. ABC was about to lay out the biggest budget ever for a television series (more than $1.5 million per episode), and the network executives were understandably reluctant to risk that much money on an actor who was an unknown and—it seemed—not much more than a brash, arrogant, New York hooligan.

Caron refused to back down, but his ABC bosses weren't budging too quickly either. For a while it seemed

Moonlighting writer/producer Glenn Gordon Caron knew at Bruce's audition that he was right for the role of David Addison. Caron believed Bruce would be "a whole new industry."

as if the whole show might be canceled outright. In the meantime, Willis lucked out and received a guest role in an episode of the new detective show *Miami Vice,* which starred Don Johnson. (Bruce played a villain—a gun smuggler with connections to the CIA.) After the filming he flew back to New York and waited. Within a day or so, Caron called Willis up on the phone and summoned him back to Hollywood: ABC had agreed to another screen test.

This time Willis cleaned himself up, got a haircut, and dressed himself in a suit and good shoes to look like a real leading man. But although Willis had gone upscale in his personal presentation, he had not lost the inner qualities that had made Caron sit up and take notice of him: that soulful machismo that came out of his working-class, macho-oriented background. From Caron's perspective Willis was more than just a fresh face on the scene. With his contradictory combination of toughness and vulnerability, sexual aggressiveness and emotional sensitivity, Willis was an antidote to the wishy-washy, overly sensitive male actors dominating the popular TV programs at that time.

The image cleanup worked: ABC offered Willis a five-year contract. The salary was a fraction of what Cybill Shepherd was being paid, but it was still more money than he'd ever seen in his life. Within a few months, when it became clear that this recently unknown actor was just as important to the show's success as his beautiful and famous costar, Willis's agent renegotiated his contracted salary to $50,000 an episode.

Bruce would later admit that he had no idea *Moonlighting* would be his big break:

> It was just another job for me. I thought, TV pilots? Dime a dozen. I thought I would do this pilot and go back to New York. But it caught on and became—boom!—this thing. It was just magic. I would hold up the original pilot against anything that's ever been on TV. It was like an

experimental theater group. We were doing something that was on the edge. There were hardly any rules. Cybill was fabulous. Particularly in the first few years, we were both really jamming.

After an iffy launch in the fall of 1985, the TV program rose like a rocket, although it would eventually crash-land five seasons later. The driving energy of the show was the almost tangible sexual tension between Dave and Maddie, co-owners of the Blue Moon Detective Agency—a friction that expressed itself only in words for the first three seasons. At first, the very macho David Addison's interest in Maddie seemed purely casual, not truly romantic or serious. But soon the role started to expand to show David's vulnerable, emotional side. Willis did a great job with this complexity. Elvis Mitchell, critic for the *New York Times,* describes one episode as follows:

In the series "Brother, Can You Spare a Blonde" episode, which gave us the first intimation of yearning in the show, the camera pans across a room from Ms. Shepherd, who is flirting and laughing with the actor playing Mr. Willis's brother, to Mr. Willis. His face torn between a glare and a grimace, he casts a look at her, tightens his mouth and looks down, an expression of frustration and dejection he'll never let her see. It's also the first time Mr. Willis got a chance to unearth something beneath the groovy young hipster arrogance. He's capable of suffering, a quality that gives weight to the bounce in his stride.

The critic goes on to say that Willis's performance proved one of the basic narrative rules of the old romantic comedies of the 1940s and 1950s, on which Caron had based his vision of the show. This premise, as the *Moonlighting* writer and producer explained, is that "feelings are all the more meaningful if you keep them to yourself." The tension and energy in the relationship between Maddie Hayes and David Addison, who kept their true desires

It wasn't long before ABC network executives realized Bruce Willis was as important to the success of Moonlighting *as its female star Cybill Shepherd. The on-screen chemistry between the two drew millions of television viewers.*

to themselves, made the show come alive for its viewers. As a boy who'd struggled hard to be able to speak, Willis probably found it very natural to portray someone who's got a lot more on his mind than he's willing to say.

As long as *Moonlighting* remained faithful to the power of unspoken, unexpressed feelings, the show was a winner with audiences worldwide. But real life intruded on show business when Cybill Shepherd—who was already growing a bit restless with her renewed fame and the intense shooting schedule required for the program— became pregnant with twins during the third season. In trying to account for the increasingly obvious pregnancy, the harried writers decided to have Maddie and Dave give in, finally, to their previously unrequited passion. This story line at the end of the third season took much of the comedic zing out of Dave and Maddie's relationship, and it confused and alienated many viewers. In the story line beginning the fourth season, Maddie left the detective agency and returned to her parents' home in Chicago. After many to-and-fro episodes, it was revealed that she was pregnant. Although it was clear that David Addison was the baby's father, for some reason Maddie decided to marry another man. This narrative twist was probably an attempt to maintain a sense of suspense and conflict, since these elements are at the heart of any good story. But if the huge volume of mail from angry and confused viewers to the ABC offices was any hint, this plot clearly did not go over very well with the audience. The show limped on through its fourth and fifth seasons, but it was never quite the same.

For Willis the show's ultimate failure didn't matter. Although his costar's three-month maternity leave put a huge dent in both the production schedule and the narrative flow of *Moonlighting,* it also afforded him time to act in other media, such as film. And it would be in movies that his rising star would be boosted out into the stratosphere: in just five years he would go from being a flat-broke bartender and struggling actor to one of the richest people on the planet.

But *Moonlighting* brought Bruce that first glimpse of fame, and his performance in the show was critically acclaimed. In 1987, he won the Golden Globe Award for Best Performance by an Actor in a Television Series (Comedy or Musical) and an Emmy for Outstanding Lead Actor in a Drama Series.

Although Bruce's role in *Moonlighting* seemed a natural fit with his personality, in his first major in-depth interview, for *Playboy* magazine, the newly famous Willis made one point clear: "I'm not David Addison. There are elements of me that are like David Addison, but he's a

In 1987 the Moonlighting *duo picked up Golden Globe Awards for Best Actor and Actress in a Television Series (Comedy or Musical).*

character." Then, in a moment that illustrates Willis's candid way of talking about himself, he goes on to confess that actually there *are* certain similarities between his own personality and that of the role he plays:

> At times, [David Addison] can be the Peter Pan of the modern world. There is a party going on inside his head and behind his eyes all the time. . . . He has a code that's sometimes mystical, sometimes very obvious. He hides behind his humor and uses it as a weapon and a shield. And ultimately, he never wants to grow up. . . . The innate part of me that is him is that fun-loving, chance-taking, risk-taking guy, who, in the face of insurmountable odds or adversity, laughs and finds a way out of it.

Willis had already shown with his speech impediment that it was possible to laugh and find a way out. Then, through a combination of luck and persistence, he'd found a way out of the impoverished life of the unknown actor. In time he would fully transform his humble, ordinary background into an actor's ability, as one critic would later describe it, "to find the contradictions in a working class man's sense of self and to wrestle with his own vulnerability."

But the Peter Pan side of Willis's personality—the eternally boyish side, the blustery, charismatic, partying side, the Bruno side—would eventually prove to be a burden as well as an asset.

The mid-1980s found the "party boy" in Bruce unleashed by success. His fame and fortune gave him the opportunity to indulge his whims and desires—and the tabloid newspapers gleefully reported on his various exploits.

6

THE PLAYER

BY DRAGGING GENE Parseghian of Triad Theatrical Agency to see her boyfriend in a play, Sheri Rivera had played an instrumental part in Bruce Willis's overnight stardom. But during the *Moonlighting* years, the ABC publicity department worked hard to keep Rivera's existence out of the press. The network was trying to maintain the titillating but false picture of a stormy off-camera romance between costars Bruce Willis and Cybill Shepherd. But Rivera had stuck by her man for three years, giving him advice and encouragement. Now, however, the very success she'd helped create was playing a part in the end of their relationship.

The main problem was Bruce's wild, rambunctious, party-boy side—the side that made him the perfect advertising spokesman for Seagram's Golden Wine Cooler, a job that was paying him $2 million a year on top of his already hefty *Moonlighting* salary. Willis had been a fun-loving guy even when he was broke. But now he had more money than he knew what to do with.

A close friend from that time, speaking anonymously to Willis's biographer, described Bruce's new life in Los Angeles:

> [I]t was the old story, repeated in this town a thousand times. When [Willis] got to Hollywood, it all changed. He was still the same guy, but the opportunities that confronted him were amazing and confusing; in that first wave of success, he went wild. Within days, they were throwing money and everything at him by the bucketful. Within months, he was getting it by the wagon load. He was also working at a terrific pace; the emotional and psychological strain was quite heavy. Everybody wanted a piece of him. Just everybody . . . publicists, managers, film people, fans and especially the media, all tearing at him. It was something of a phenomenon, even for this mad, bad town.

Bruce had the kind of fame and money he hadn't dared dream about when he was shuttling workers around the DuPont plant just 10 years earlier. After working long hours on the set of *Moonlighting,* he'd go out drinking with his buddies until all hours of the morning and have maudlin conversations about his sudden fame and wealth. Why me? he'd ask. The unexpected celebrity must have baffled him, must have threatened his long-standing image of himself as a "regular guy." As his friend put it, "It sounds almost pathetic to say that, for a fleeting moment, you could actually feel sorry for the guy. That's a ridiculous thought, isn't it? Who could, really? He had choices now, and as Michael Douglas once said, power in Hollywood means having choices. But I could understand his confusion."

When Sheri left him toward the end of 1986, Willis lost his one major anchor to a stable lifestyle. He immediately entered a phase that he'd later call his "swinging bachelor days." He bought a house in Nichols Canyon, a quiet neighborhood in the Hollywood hills off Mulholland Drive, not too far from the homes of two "bad boys" from an earlier Hollywood generation, Jack Nicholson and Marlon Brando. Willis specifically looked for a place large enough, and far enough from his neighbors, to accommodate loud parties. The house he chose was on six acres, nestled within its own little canyon. In an interview, Willis enthused about his new home:

> I fantasized this conversation I would have with my neighbors: "Oh, hi, Mr. Willis. What are those structures down there at the bottom of the canyon, guesthouses?"
>
> "No, they ain't guesthouses."
>
> "What are they?"
>
> "Speakers."

Willis offered another story about his partying life at the Nichols Canyon house:

> I had this stereo; the volume control went from zero to ten. One night, I yelled to my friends, "Turn it up!"
>
> "We can't, Bruce, it's on ten."
>
> So we got a big butane lighter and tried to burn the little plastic piece above the volume control, so we could push the volume up higher. I did like to play the music loud.

At first Willis seemed to be a "nice, regular guy," as one neighbor put it. Within a few months, though, nearby residents began to complain about the loud parties. The first few times there were complaints, Willis was considerate enough to turn down the volume when asked. But then he started to get arrogant about the whole business. The standoff between Willis and his neighbors came to a head on Memorial Day, 1987, at a huge pool party he was throwing in honor of his new friend, an actor also known for troublemaking—Sean Penn.

Willis's outdoor party was so loud, the sounds of R&B music could be heard several streets away. Around ten o'clock at night some police officers showed up at the front door. When no one answered the doorbell, the officers went around the back way and straight into the house. According to Lieutenant Neil Zachary, who compiled the official police report on the incident for the Los Angeles

Ignoring the questions of an inquisitive reporter, Willis arrives at the Hollywood courthouse following his arrest in May 1987. Police had responded to complaints of loud music at Willis's home, where a confrontation between the officers and Bruce resulted in his arrest.

Police Department, Willis reacted violently when he saw them in his home. He came "rushing at the officers, arms outstretched and yelling abusive language at them . . . demanding to know why they had walked into his house without being invited . . . he said he wouldn't talk to them until they got out of his house . . . and then [he] attempted to push one of the officers out."

Willis would relay a slightly different version of the same story:

> By the time I got out of the pool, this one cop was already in my house, and I asked him why he was there. I said, "I won't talk to you until you get out of my house," because he didn't have a warrant and I felt invaded. And it just

escalated. I was cursing at him and he took offense—this guy was sensitive. He said, "I've arrested more important people than *you*. You think you're going to get away with all this?" All we were doing was *dancing*—But the cop had a point to make. His point was, actors are not above the law.

Regardless of who was actually at fault—Willis, for using foul and abusive language, or the police, for entering the house without a warrant and overreacting to the situation—the end result of this encounter was that Willis was arrested. As he later explained, it was a painful experience in more than one way: "I had a broken shoulder at the time, and my friends tried to tell [the police officer] about it. He put the handcuffs on me and cranked my arm up around my back, like you see on TV. I heard it go *snick, snick, snick*—it broke again. And it was chaos. I was yelling in pain, my friends were yelling that I was in pain, and the cop felt threatened, so he called in more cops."

In the continuing chaos half a dozen police cars came to the house. Five men, including Willis and his younger brother Robert, were arrested and put in the local jail for more than two hours, on charges of assaulting a police officer. Meanwhile, Willis was in so much pain, the police agreed to take him to a local hospital for treatment. As excruciating as the reinjury was, it was a lucky break in one way, because it allowed Willis's lawyers to argue that the police had been "overzealous" in their arrest. According to some sources, Willis's lawyers also threatened to sue the police department over the injury. Eventually all charges against him and the four other men were dropped.

Willis moved out of Nichols Canyon the night of his arrest and relocated to a $3 million Malibu beach house that had just been built for him. But his wild parties did not stop—nor did the trouble with police and the press. Just a few weeks after Bruce moved to the beach house, the body of a young man who had drowned in the sea was found

In his first starring role in a movie, Bruce played opposite Kim Basinger in Blake Edwards's 1987 film Blind Date. *The comedy was panned by critics, but did well at the box office.*

nearby. Evidently he had been either attending a Willis party or helping to fix one of the star's Jet Skis. The circumstances were never fully cleared up, but in the end the man's death was ruled accidental. This, however, did not keep the press—specifically, the sleazy tabloid newspapers—from labeling the episode a "mystery," hinting at foul play on Willis's part, and predicting the star's certain downfall when the allegedly horrible truth was revealed. Needless to say, that day never came.

Years later Willis would be partly apologetic and partly defensive about his lifestyle during those days. He told one interviewer, "[The] whole [Nichols Canyon] incident with the police was just God's way of saying slow down. Me and my friends lived like we were 16 and had money. We were reliving our youth. And I defy you to find any man who—if given that opportunity—would not take advantage of it. At that time, I was just having everything handed to me. I was like a kid who was never given anything and then given a toy store and told, 'It's all yours.' There's no mystery to living like that, to living hard and partying."

At the same time he was "living hard," Willis was quickly becoming one of the most sought-after actors in Hollywood. He made his movie debut in *Blind Date* (1987), a comedy about a woman, played by Kim Basinger, who goes crazy if she drinks even a drop of alcohol. As her completely sober date for the evening, Willis plays against type—in a role that is quite the opposite of how he was conducting his own life at the time. *Blind Date* was widely panned by critics, but on the strength of Willis's fame it grossed $87 million at the box office anyway.

When Bruce was offered a starring part in Stanley Kubrick's *Full Metal Jacket* (1987), he had to turn it down because that job conflicted with the *Moonlighting* production schedule. Soon enough he'd star in his second film— the murder-mystery farce *Sunset* (1988). In the movie, which is set in 1920s Hollywood, Willis plays cowboy star Tom Mix, who helps out legendary marshal Wyatt Earp, played by James Garner. But like *Blind Date,* the film was poorly received.

And then, just three years after arriving in Hollywood, Willis was asked to play New York City detective John McClane, the battered and bruised hero of *Die Hard* (1988) and the first big-screen character to make use of Willis's particular brand of regular-guy machismo. Willis was at first a little reluctant to take the picture. He was aspiring to be a real movie actor, not the kind of Teflon-coated, one-dimensional action hero that Sylvester Stallone and Arnold Schwarzenegger had become.

To entice this man of the moment, the producers of *Die Hard* offered the actor $5 million, then one of the highest fees ever paid to an actor for a single movie, no matter how famous. And it was a whopping amount for a relative newcomer. Only the big stars were offered such huge salaries. As biographer John Parker puts it, "It was

Although a forgettable movie by most critics' standards, Bruce's second film, Sunset *(1988), offered him the chance to work with the renowned actor James Garner.*

Brando money. Even Jack Nicholson, the master of that era, only received $5 million for *Witches of Eastwick* in the same year. Sean Connery, Dustin Hoffman and Matthew Broderick shared less than $10 million for *Family Business.* De Niro was struggling to make $2 million a picture. Even Stallone and Schwarzenegger were only hovering around the fee Willis would get from *Die Hard.*"

So Willis must have felt like the king of the world. At the same time, he probably knew his wild-boy days were numbered. Part of his agreement to do *Die Hard* involved a pledge that during the filming he'd stop partying, he'd start attending sessions of Alcoholics Anonymous, and there would be no incidents involving broken shoulders, arrests, or any reasons for the tabloid press to hound him.

At the same time, *Moonlighting* was dying a slow, agonizing death, in terms of both the viewers' response and the cast's enthusiasm. Although the newspaper tabloids had fabricated the tales of fistfights between the costars, it was true that tensions on the set were mounting, as both Willis and Shepherd began to regret the long, five-year contract they'd signed to do the show. In 1988, Willis described the relationship between the two of them:

> I don't think either of us has a shorter fuse than the other. I've been known to go off at the drop of a hat, and so has she. But a lot of that's mellowed. . . . [W]e've created a body of work that we are both very proud of. It's like a marriage, a forced marriage. We have to work with each other, because we have contracts, no matter how we feel about each other. And I'll admit, there were days when I'd come to work and I did not want to work with her. Did not want to talk to her.

All in all, the late 1980s were crazy, hectic, wildly successful, but somewhat confusing years for Willis, both professionally and personally. At some point toward the end of the decade Bruce would scale back on his drinking and partying, and he would even decide to enter psychotherapy treatment to try to iron out some of the continuing self-esteem issues that he'd been harboring since his days as a stutterer and the child of unhappily married parents.

Soon, though, he'd meet the person who'd put a definitive end to his Peter Pan ways. True, she'd had plenty of trouble becoming a grown-up herself. But together they'd find the strength to emerge from their drunken, irresponsible pasts and become one of Hollywood's most powerful couples.

Bruce Willis accompanies his wife, Demi Moore, at the 1989 Academy Awards. With marriage to Demi in 1987 and a movie contract that required him to amend his reckless lifestyle, Bruce began to settle down.

7

MORTAL THOUGHTS

IN THE LATE 1980s there were two major factors motivating Bruce Willis to amend his hard-drinking, loud-music ways: his new relationship with Demi Moore and his contract with producer Joel Silver to do the movie *Die Hard.*

Demi Moore had been through her own wild-child phase and had already worked hard to change her ways several years before she met Bruce Willis. She'd been raised chaotically by an alcoholic mother and a suicidal, con-artist father, who later turned out not to be Demi's true biological father. As a child, Demi had also had a physical adversity to overcome: she was extremely cross-eyed, a condition that required two operations to correct.

At age 16, Demi quit school and left her Roswell, New Mexico, home for Los Angeles. She married and then divorced a rock musician, posed nude for a men's magazine, beat out 1,000 actresses to win a recurring role in the soap opera *General Hospital,* and struggled with drug and alcohol addiction—all before turning 21 years old. Demi Moore's big break came in 1984, when she was cast as a glamorous, rich, but unhappy and cocaine-addicted college girl in the film *St. Elmo's Fire.* It was a part for which the director, Joel Schumacher, had interviewed more than 500 actresses. Moore's success over such a large field was very much like Willis's own unlikely triumph that year over the 3,000 actors who were screened for the *Moonlighting* job. As in Willis's case, the director was absolutely convinced that he'd found the perfect person for the part. But Demi almost botched her big opportunity when she staggered in drunk to her wardrobe fitting. Schumacher told her she needed to clean up her act or she would be fired.

With Moore's full consent, Schumacher convinced the producers to pay for her to enter a residential substance-abuse treatment program during the rehearsal period. She completed the program and later began attending meetings with the 12-step program Adult Children of Alcoholics (ACOA). Little by little, Demi Moore's life came under her control. As it did, other parts of her strong personality began to emerge: her ambition, her drive, her willingness to fight hard for what she wanted.

During this recovery period Demi Moore became involved with Emilio Estevez, the son of Martin Sheen and a member of the "Brat Pack," a generation of young actors who had a reputation for living and partying hard. After a three-year on-and-off relationship with Estevez, Moore had just broken off their engagement when she met Willis at the screening of Estevez's new movie, *Stakeout,* in 1987. After just a three-month courtship, Willis and Moore were married in Las Vegas by a justice of the peace. Three weeks later, on November 21, they held a second wedding in Hollywood, this time a glamorous, celebrity-filled ceremony for 450 invited guests, presided over by the rock 'n' roll legend (and ordained minister) Little Richard. The gala cost nearly a million dollars.

At the beginning of their relationship Bruce was exactly where Demi had been years earlier: facing an ultimatum to shape up or ship out. As a condition of his $5 million contract with the producers of *Die Hard,* Willis had to clean up his act, just as his new mate had done three years earlier. With the help of counselors and Demi, Bruce stopped drinking entirely. Eventually he also came to a mutual agreement with Seagram's to stop being its spokesperson and stop making commercials for the Golden Wine Cooler. He later said, "I felt that I could not morally promote something that I didn't do any longer myself."

Around this time Willis also began seeing a pschotherapist. In a 1988 interview he talked about his therapy sessions:

> In the past eight months, I've really been challenging myself, making myself look at things that I refused to look at for a long, long time. About my childhood. It's very easy not to look at those things; it takes courage [to face them]. I've spent a huge part of my life so far with self-constructed walls around me, to protect myself from myself. I've gotten brave enough to start knocking them down, but they are not all down yet, not by any means.

When asked what exactly his childhood had lacked, Willis responded, "I don't remember there being a lot of closeness in my family. There was a lot of isolation, separation. There wasn't a lot of hugging going on." A few years after that interview he'd be given an opportunity that many adults with unhappy childhoods dream of: the chance to try avoiding his parents' mistakes when he began his own family.

In 1987, Bruce also began a challenging fitness regimen meant to turn his slack, party-boy body into a sleek machine. The *Die Hard* producers didn't want to transform him into a muscle-bound giant like Stallone or Schwarzenegger. They wanted him to retain his ordinary-guy appearance to play Detective John McClane, an off-duty New York City police detective who ends up battling a crowd of murderous terrorists who have taken over the Los Angeles office building in which his ex-wife works.

The 1988 film Die Hard *earned Bruce a cool $5 million, as well as a reputation as an action hero. As New York City police detective John McClane, Bruce created an appealing character—an ordinary man who can successfully deal with an extraordinarily dangerous situation.*

Willis didn't need to become a muscle-rippling character like Schwarzenegger's Terminator, but he did need to look at least credible in the part, which involved some intense stunts and acrobatics. So he cut out the junk food in favor of a high-protein, high-fiber diet with lots of fruits and vegetables, and began two months of intensive work with weights to build up his chest and arms.

From all these emotional and physical workouts, the cumulative result was a new Bruce Willis: taut, serious, tamed, and—in the company of his extremely ambitious and focused wife—even more driven than before.

Detective John McClane, Willis's character in *Die Hard,* was a near-perfect role for him. McClane was not a Rambo-style superman, but a vulnerable, terrified, ordinary man who had been thrust into an extremely dangerous situation. With its many explosions and special effects, *Die Hard* was definitely an action picture. But Willis's surprisingly nuanced characterization gave the film an unexpected depth. Critics and audiences were equally impressed; the film was a blockbuster from its first weekend in the theaters. Willis became one of the few actors ever to make such a truly successful leap from television to the movies. With the critical and commercial success of *Die Hard,* the disappointments of *Blind Date* and *Sunset* were soon forgotten.

But as always, success came with a potentially high price. Willis continued to think of himself as a serious actor, not a one-dimensional action hero. Now that he had proved himself worthy of a $5 million price tag, however, directors of smaller, more complicated films were scared off from hiring him for their productions. In response, Willis's new agent, Arnold Rifkin, encouraged his client to adopt the following policy: the actor would accept the big-money roles in blockbuster action pictures, but in between he would make himself available for much smaller fees, or even no money up front, to be cast in interesting movies.

This strategy was evident in Willis's choices for his next two movies. He portrayed a traumatized Vietnam War veteran in the film *In Country* (1989). In the small, quiet drama Emily Lloyd plays a young girl who contacts her estranged uncle, played by Willis, in hopes of learning about her father, who had died in Vietnam. Bruce was paid very little for his part in the production, but he worked hard, researched his role, and turned in a remarkable performance. However, the film was not financially successful. In contrast, for the box-office hit *Look Who's Talking* (1989), Willis expended very little effort providing the voice of the cynical, witty baby Mikey, and was paid a great deal of money.

Unfortunately, these two movies set an undesirable precedent in terms of how viewers responded to Willis's choices. As a *New York Times* film critic observed, "For some reason, whenever Mr. Willis underplays and shows some sophistication as an actor, he is, for the most part, ignored." The critic went on to praise Willis for avoiding the "exhibitionistic explosiveness that's a stock reaction for actors in such [roles]." Instead of portraying the Vietnam veteran as a violent, volatile character, the writer commented, Willis had chosen to play him as "a man who's lost in his own skin, and is past caring how others think of him." But very few people bothered to go see *In Country,* perhaps because of its rather depressing subject matter. It would take several more years—and a lot of complete bombs—before Willis would begin to find movies that combined challenging, interesting characters and story lines with the great potential to attract big audiences.

Meanwhile, Willis and Moore were busy trying to protect the privacy of their marriage and their growing family. Tabloid press reporters hounded them constantly. Willis once got into an altercation with an aggressive photographer who'd caused Moore, then four months pregnant, to stumble and fall. Soon after their wedding, the couple purchased a home in the tiny town of Hailey, Idaho. Although they continued to maintain residences near Hollywood and in New York City, Bruce and Demi began to center their life in this quiet, rural, extremely private location, far from the "paparazzi"—freelance photographers in search of candid celebrity shots.

With the responsibilities of fatherhood, Bruce may have finally tamed his wild side. Here he holds his newborn daughter Tallulah Belle; Willis has worked hard to be a good father to all three of his daughters.

On August 16, 1988, during the filming of *In Country,* the couple's first daughter was born and named Rumer Glenn, after the British author Rumer Godden. Remembering the lack of intimacy in his own family, Willis worked hard to be the kind of parent he wished he'd been blessed with, beginning with being actively involved in his daughter's birth. Within a few years Rumer had two sisters to keep her company: Scout Larue (named for the narrator of the novel *To Kill a Mockingbird*), born on July 20, 1991, and Tallulah Belle (named after legendary actress Tallulah Bankhead), born on February 3, 1994. Bruce would prove to be a very devoted, loving father to all his children.

In 1988, just before Rumer's birth, Willis had predicted in an interview that having kids would be good for him: "[It will] make me a little more mellow. It makes me want to get out of TV, so I can go play with my kid. I would like now to take a couple of years off, Demi can go to work if she wants. I have no problem with that at all." With his new mellow, family-oriented, surprisingly nonchauvinist lifestyle, Willis finally seemed ready to grow up and leave his Bruno persona behind forever.

In a second in-depth interview with *Playboy* magazine, the father of three explained how he now had his own mortal thoughts—how fatherhood had made him more responsible: "I still do dangerous things, but I have cut way down. I have a much stronger awareness of my own mortality. I'm much more careful than I used to be. I wear a helmet when I ride my motorcycle. I don't need my kids saying, 'Oh, Daddy fell off his motorcycle and cracked his head open. Now we have no more Daddy.' I consider the consequences of things, which I never did before."

Although Bruce had settled down as a family man, that didn't necessarily mean his life would stop being a rollercoaster ride in one way or another.

A scene from Bruce Willis's HBO special The Return of Bruno. *In the documentary of a fictional rock-and-roll singer named Bruno Radolini, Bruce performs songs that also appear on his Motown album. Celebrity allowed Bruce to indulge himself with a bit of moonlighting—that is, holding jobs as a singer and television performer in addition to his regular work as a movie actor.*

8

MOONLIGHTING

MOST CREATIVE PEOPLE seem to have talents and interests in more than one field of endeavor. Even if they focus intensely on one activity, they may find themselves with a desire to moonlight—in other words, to focus on a second or even third career side by side with the first one.

What happens when you become rich and famous, however, is that you get to indulge these secondary talents and interests, to stretch yourself in new directions, in ways that may not have been possible if you were still obscure and impoverished. If you're already a famous movie director like Woody Allen, you can get yourself a once-a-week gig as a jazz clarinetist in a New York City restaurant, even if there are a thousand unknown musicians out there who are as good as you. If you're already an action hero like Sylvester Stallone, or a beloved, world-famous singer like Frank Sinatra, you can take up painting in your middle age and find people who want to buy your work at rather inflated prices, regardless of the actual artistic value. If you are a powerful person, it's only natural to want to use your position and influence to get to do the things you really enjoy.

Bruce Willis is one of the lucky few human beings who has the financial resources and the practical power to follow his dreams wherever they might lead. But having the money and contacts doesn't guarantee that those dreams will always turn out as planned.

In his high school yearbook Willis—who at the time had not yet set a goal to be an actor—wrote that his only ambitions in life were to "become deliriously happy, or a professional harp player." By *harp,* of course, he meant mouth harp or harmonica—not the huge, gilt, stringed instruments you see in classical orchestras. A little more than 10 years later Bruce fulfilled at least part of his wish.

An executive with Motown Records—the African American-run company specializing in the soul and R&B music that Willis practically worshiped as a child—had been watching *Moonlighting.* He had noticed that David Addison often started singing and would even occasionally play his harmonica on the program. On the basis of these TV performances, the record company head approached Willis and offered him a contract.

So during the summer of 1986, Willis went into the Motown Records studio with a coterie of top-line musicians, including members of the 1960s and 1970s soul super-group the Temptations. Together they recorded blues and soul standards such as "Under the Boardwalk," "Secret Agent Man," and "Respect Yourself."

Willis knew he had a pretty ordinary voice—and so did music critics, who roundly dismissed him as a fraud or a novelty act. But the Motown album, entitled *The Return of Bruno,* went platinum (sold more than 1 million copies), and "Respect Yourself" actually made it onto the charts as a hit single. Willis soon got the opportunity to perform in front of audiences ranging in size from 20,000 to 30,000 people. That's the kind of audience most first-time recording artists can only dream of.

Bruce probably heads the list of his most severe critics when it comes to evaluating his singing ability:

I've never been really happy with the sound of my voice. I'm more a hollerer than a singer. Sinatra sings, I holler loudly in key. . . . [M]y album ended up doing well; but if I had my way, I would have scrapped a bunch of the stuff on the album and started over with my new knowledge about how to approach it. But I would have done the album for free; it was just a fun thing to do.

Having built-in fame doesn't guarantee success in all endeavors. In the case of *The Return of Bruno,* things had worked out pretty well: after all, when Willis accepted the contract with Motown Records, he knew he wasn't headed for any kind of serious musical career. Despite the poor critical response, the album itself was a huge financial success for him and for the record company.

Bruce poses with three of his four partners in the Planet Hollywood restaurant business—Arnold Schwarzenegger (left), Demi Moore, and Sylvester Stallone. Although extremely popular for the first few years, the movie-themed restaurant chain came close to bankruptcy in 1999.

Bruce's first attempt at film production was Hudson Hawk, *which simply didn't fly with movie-goers. Critics knocked the film for its incredibly unrealistic plot and for serving as little more than a vehicle for Bruce's wisecracking humor.*

Five years later Willis followed up with a second Motown album, with the autobiographical title, *If It Don't Kill You, It Just Makes You Stronger.* The R&B album would not be as financially successful as his first one. And other Willis projects would also not turn out so well.

In 1991, Willis became one of the five celebrities—along with Demi Moore, Whoopi Goldberg, Sylvester Stallone, and Arnold Schwarzenegger—to become shareholders and partners in a new movie-themed restaurant chain venture called Planet Hollywood. Willis and his famous partners would receive a slice of the profits in exchange for lending their names to the company, appearing at grand openings, and helping generate as much publicity as possible for the restaurants. That same year the first Planet Hollywood opened in New York City with the five celebrity partners in attendance. They mingled with guests and signed autographs, and Willis even did a bit of singing.

Within a few years Planet Hollywood had opened dozens of locations around the country and the world, often in high-traffic, tourist-filled areas in places like Orlando, Florida; Las Vegas, Nevada; London, England; and Paris, France. Although the food was never anything to write home about, people flocked to the restaurants, in part to gawk at or buy the restaurant decorations—props, costumes, and other movie memorabilia that had been taken from the sets of blockbuster pictures, such as Willis's *Die Hard,* Harrison Ford's *Raiders of the Lost Ark,* and Arnold Schwarzenegger's *Terminator.*

Ultimately, though, the restaurant business is a very tough one, with high risk and low profit margins, and even a roster of famous shareholders can't necessarily hold failure at bay forever. By the mid-1990s many of the chain's outlets were struggling to stay profitable, despite their star-studded promotional backing. The restaurant chain's stock value roller-coastered up and down. In August 1999, Planet Hollywood planned to file for bankruptcy, although by early 2000 it seemed that a new plan to reorganize the company would keep it from going under completely. As Planet Hollywood's stockholders learned, fame may be powerful, but it isn't invincible.

Furthermore, fame brings its own challenges and liabilities. Once actors hit the big time, every move they make within the movie industry is scrutinized. Critics can be particularly hard on actors who try to take more control over their projects by becoming writers, producers, or directors of films. Some performers—Clint Eastwood, Robert De Niro, and Barbra Streisand come to mind—do a very reasonable job of expanding their roles to have more creative control over the movies they make. Others don't have as much luck, or don't demonstrate as much skill or business sense.

And then some actors make the mistake of getting stuck on a childhood dream project that really should have remained a dream. Willis's big mistake was *Hudson Hawk* (1991). For years he'd been talking about making his own movie, but although he'd been buying the rights to scripts and books, nothing had panned out. So he decided to use a script that he'd written years ago while living in New York. The story was subsequently worked on by another scriptwriter, and plans moved ahead. Willis, who would star in the movie, became closely involved with the film's production as well.

Hudson Hawk is an amateurish, Indiana Jones–style adventure caper about a famous cat burglar recently released from prison who is then blackmailed into stealing artwork. From the start Willis was hopelessly unrealistic about this movie's potential. At the premiere party for *Die Hard 2: Die Harder* (1990), the sequel to his first blockbuster film, *Die Hard,* he boasted, "We'll be bringing home a great movie—bigger than *Die Harder.*"

To make such grandiose predictions is almost to guarantee failure, particularly in Hollywood, where the press corps regularly tries to cut boasters down to size. True, when the film finally came out in 1991—after a ludicrously expensive production ($61 million, way over budget) full of delays and problems—the critics were perhaps a little too hostile and merciless. Having loudly proclaimed his great expectations, Willis had set everybody up for terrible disappointment. But it wasn't only critics who hated the movie: audiences (who often don't listen to critics) stayed away in droves.

There's also a large personal downside to being rich, famous, and instantly recognizable. To get away from aggressive tabloid reporters and the continually flashing cameras of the paparazzi, Bruce Willis and Demi Moore had retreated in the late 1980s to the rural town of Hailey, Idaho. It was a sleepy former gold-rush town, containing one main street and an official population of about 3,500.

Until Willis and Moore arrived, Hailey had mostly been ignored by passersby, even though it was just 12 miles away from Sun Valley, a major ski-resort town and popular playground of the rich and famous. On the town outskirts Willis and Moore purchased a six-bedroom ranch house set on 25 acres.

Although some longtime Hailey residents were worried that their hometown would suddenly be overrun by tourists hoping to catch a glimpse of the famous couple, most came to the conclusion that Willis and Moore were "just ordinary folk with money." The problem was, although they claimed to want to live a normal, glitz-free life, they couldn't keep from using their money and power to bring about some major changes in the town—changes, but not necessarily improvements. "The trappings of celebrity proved harder to shake off than Willis and Moore might have anticipated," as one London newspaper

Of all his outside business attempts, Bruce probably has most enjoyed jamming and performing before Planet Hollywood crowds.

reporter put it. "Instead of blending into the landscape—
the great fantasy that has lured celebrities to Idaho's Sun
Valley area for the past half-century—the glamorous couple found it hard to resist the temptation to put their own
stamp on their surroundings."

Surely, Willis and Moore began with good intentions.
They redeveloped an old launderette into an elegant
redbrick shopping center and office building, with a
1950s-style diner, named Shorty's, on the first floor. They
rehabilitated an old movie theater, giving it plush seating
and a multimillion-dollar sound system. They rebuilt a
dingy dive bar called the Mint and transformed it into a
nightclub featuring famous national acts such as R&B
guitarists B. B. King and Bo Diddley—performers who
probably would never have bothered booking gigs in a
small town like Hailey, were it not for the very famous
and powerful hosts.

Soon enough, Hailey became a boomtown, filled with
tourists and celebrities. But there was one fundamental
problem: without Bruce Willis and Demi Moore the town
did not have an underlying economy that could support
this kind of business activity. Besides, the success of
Willis's ventures meant that other businesses—some run
by people who'd lived in Hailey all their lives—would fail.
For example, Shorty's was so popular that it drove the
other two older diners in Hailey out of business.

It's unhealthy and risky for any town, city, state, or
country to be dependent on one single industry for its economic livelihood. In Hailey's case Bruce Willis had
become the one industry. By the mid-1990s his local real
estate company, Valley Entertainment, employed 250 people, or almost 10 percent of the town's permanent population. But then, in 1999, personal problems would have a
sudden and negative effect on his business dealings. That
year Willis abruptly closed down Shorty's and the Mint,
firing everyone who worked there with no explanation. He
also left a good amount of unfinished work in Hailey: two

half-developed, empty buildings on Main Street and unrealized plans for a children's recreation center and swimming pool. Needless to say, Willis's shocking and sudden actions shook the town's economy to its core.

The Hailey situation reminded many of a similar incident from a few years earlier, back in Willis's old stomping grounds of Penns Grove, New Jersey. In 1995, Willis had bought 11 acres of land along the Delaware River and announced his plans to use the site for a $50 million development with a marina, hotel, and theaters. Such news thrilled the people of Penns Grove, who had watched their town slowly lose its industrial base over the decades, until it had become the second-poorest town in the state. Two years after making this announcement, however, Willis lost interest in the project—for reasons that were never fully divulged to the public—and put the land up for sale. Understandably, many Penns Grove residents were deeply disappointed, perhaps even devastated.

As an American businessman, Willis of course has every right to run his enterprises as he sees fit. He is certainly not the first real estate mogul to behave in capricious or seemingly unpredictable ways that cause economic hardships for other, less powerful people. In both Penns Grove and Hailey, Willis may have had perfectly good reasons for acting the way he did—reasons that have not been revealed to the public.

For better or worse, however, movie stars attract a lot more attention to themselves than most real estate developers do. Willis may be no more or less guilty than any other businessman of occasionally disappointing the expectations of his employees and customers. But the fact remains: ordinary people pay close attention to what celebrities like Willis and Moore are doing with their money, time, and power. Such is the danger of fame.

Bruce's career has been as volatile as mercury. As he explains, "There's basically four stories they can write about you. One: You hit the scene. Two: You peak. Three: You bomb. And four: You come back."

9

MERCURY RISING

SO BRUCE WILLIS IS clearly not particularly successful as a musician, film producer, restaurateur, or real estate developer. But then there's simply Bruce Willis, the actor. Like most Hollywood stars, he has made some bad script choices on occasion and as a result has appeared in some truly forgettable movies. But unlike his fellow action-flick heroes and Planet Hollywood partners, Stallone and Schwarzenegger, Willis has actually been able to demonstrate a surprising amount of growth and depth as a character actor. In some ways he's been able to fulfill both of Glenn Gordon Caron's prophecies: he's become a one-man, multimillion-dollar industry, but he's also become a strong leading man—a charming, charismatic, eloquent, opinionated, multifaceted type reminiscent of the classic actors of previous generations, like Marlon Brando, Cary Grant, and Jimmy Stewart.

Willis—the kid who practically dared other children to laugh at him for his stutter, the kid who streaked naked through the center of town, the kid who spurned his college drama professors and went his own way—has continued to be a risk taker. From 1988 on, he has maintained his policy of trying to alternate big-money action pictures with lower-budget dramas and comedies, although it hasn't always been easy. In the early 1990s, Willis found himself a bit constricted by his own success. His big-money sequels, *Die Hard 2* and *Look Who's Talking Too* (1990), did well at the box office, but soon afterward Willis took on one ill-fated project after another, and his career virtually stalled for a while.

One of the first of these unsuccessful films was *The Bonfire of the Vanities* (1990), based on the best-selling novel by Tom Wolfe about greed and corruption in 1980s New York City. The story was adapted by director Brian De Palma, who at the time was best known for thrillers and crime movies such as *Carrie* (1976), *Body Double* (1984), and *The Untouchables* (1987). Since so many people had read and loved Wolfe's book, the filmmakers were working against very high expectations from the beginning. But they failed to meet those expectations, particularly because De Palma was not able to capture the way the novelist had delved so deeply into his main character's thoughts.

Furthermore, the three stars chosen for the leads were miscast. Tom Hanks plowed unconvincingly through the troubles of Sherman McCoy, a rich white investment banker involved in a hit-and-run car accident in which a black teenager is killed. Melanie Griffith, fresh from her triumph in *Working Girl* (1988), couldn't really handle the Southern accent required for her part as Sherman McCoy's mistress. And Willis, in the role of corrupt, heavy-drinking journalist Peter Fallow, "ambled through the story in typical conversational style but provided little in the way of verbal elegance or insight," according to biographer John Parker. The film, which cost $40 million to make, bombed at the box office.

Willis took his $3 million fee for that movie and tried to move forward. But then he got stuck in a number of other ill-conceived and poorly executed projects: his own *Hudson Hawk,* and *Billy Bathgate* (1991), based on E. L.

Doctorow's novel about the 1930s gangster Dutch Schultz. Next, in *The Last Boy Scout* (1991), Willis played a fired Secret Service agent-turned-detective. The film was an extremely violent movie that attracted Willis's core audience of action-movie lovers, but it did nothing to further his own goals as a character actor. In 1992, Bruce made a brief but well-received cameo appearance in Robert Altman's cynical black comedy about Hollywood, *The Player,* which starred Tim Robbins. Still, that was really just a walk-on role.

At this particular time, in the early 1990s, both Demi Moore and Bruce Willis were favorite targets of tabloid reporters and film critics alike—sometimes for good reason. Their behavior in public often seemed arrogant and pretentious: they once walked into a fancy restaurant with a half dozen bodyguards. Over the years Moore had become particularly infamous for hiring huge, expensive support staffs (nannies, cooks, physical trainers, makeup artists, hairdressers) whenever she was on location filming—more helpers than even the most indulgent megastar bothers to bring along, according to press accounts.

Although Willis and Moore complained, as all stars do, about the media constantly intruding on their privacy, they were not unwilling to take advantage of publicity when it suited their needs. Moore, in particular, had a tendency to flaunt her nearly-naked body on magazine covers and late-night TV shows when promoting her movies. This kind of exhibitionism actually worked to generate huge amounts of publicity for her films, but it also made her vulnerable to the charge that she wasn't a real actress, just a pretty face and a well-toned body.

In reality, Moore was attempting to be not just a serious actress, but also a serious power broker in Hollywood. Spurred on by her husband's producing venture with *Hudson Hawk,* she was eager to be in charge of her own films. So she formed an independent company, quickly finding willing financial backers. Her easy success turned heads; it usually took even well-known actors years and years to obtain enough money for their pet film projects. But Moore was riding high after her acclaimed performance in *Ghost* (1990), a phenomenally successful movie about a woman whose beloved boyfriend, played by Patrick Swayze, comes back from the dead to protect her from his murderer.

Moore's role as the "boss lady" garnered her some additional bad press. Her response was typically concise and combative: "There are too many good actresses around to fill the roles for women. So you have to go out there and fight, pay attention, know what's going on. The reality is you have to generate roles for yourself. That's right, and nobody will stop me now."

With those fighting words Moore charged ahead as coproducer and star of *Mortal Thoughts* (1991), a bleak but effective suspense thriller costarring her husband, Bruce Willis, as a violent drunkard and wife beater. Although the movie was not compelling enough to make it a big success at the box office, the film did demonstrate Willis's willingness to take on a relatively risky, difficult role.

Willis took another big risk with *Death Becomes Her* (1992), a bizarre slapstick comedy about two vain, feuding women, played by Goldie Hawn and Meryl Streep, who drink an elixir that makes them immortal. They then proceed to bash and shoot at each other, which causes broken limbs and all sorts of other ugly trauma but doesn't kill them. Taking on a role that was against type, Willis played the unattractive, bespectacled, soft-spoken plastic surgeon who must keep patching up the ever-feuding, decaying immortal bodies. It was a one-joke movie, and that joke wore thin pretty quickly, despite the film's rather astonishing special effects. Willis turned in a surprisingly smirk-free performance that hinted of better things to come.

After practically sleepwalking his way through another action film, called *Striking Distance* (1993)—jokingly referred to by some as "Die Hard on a Police Boat"—Willis hit dramatic pay dirt when his friend and fellow

actor Harvey Keitel introduced him to new wunderkind writer/director Quentin Tarantino at a barbecue at Keitel's house. Tarantino had written a new script, an inventive, original, very violent but oddly funny story called *Pulp Fiction* (1994). Although Tarantino could pay him only the union scale amount for actors (about $1,000 per filming day), Willis agreed to take the part because he thought the script was great.

In *Pulp Fiction,* Willis was cast as Butch Coolidge, a corrupt boxer who gets paid off by a gangster to throw a fight (that is, to deliberately lose so that gamblers can make money betting on his opponent). However, Butch decides to win it anyway and actually ends up accidentally killing his opponent in the ring. He then has to go on the run to avoid being assassinated by the gangster who'd paid him. In a

Demi Moore coproduced and starred in the suspense thriller Mortal Thoughts, *which also starred husband Bruce Willis. In the film, Bruce demonstrates his range as an actor, playing the difficult role of a violent, abusive alcoholic.*

Terry Gilliam's science fiction film 12 Monkeys *received positive reviews both for its plot and the part Bruce played. The story line involved an interesting twist on time travel in the past, present, and future.*

strange and violent twist of fate, Coolidge gets a chance to save the gangster's life, thereby erasing his "debt" to the man. Willis's role was just a supporting part in a rather large and star-studded cast ensemble, but Bruce proved once again to audiences and critics alike that he was capable of portraying a complex, contradictory male character—someone who is strong but vulnerable, violent but tender, corrupt but principled. Gone were the smirks, the jokes, and the cavalier wit of Willis's youth. Bruno was nowhere to be found.

As he told an interviewer later on, Willis—a lifelong reader—was drawn in by the excellent writing in Tarantino's script:

> [T]he dialogue was perfect. There's so much real life in this wild story—that's what I like about it. The speech I have with Maria de Medeiros [who plays Butch's girlfriend] at the end is an example. I've just gone through this hellacious

morning—worst morning of my life—and we have to get out of town. But I have to take the time to ask her about her breakfast—did she get blueberry pancakes like she wanted? I know every guy in America understood that moment. I'm dying, my nose is broken, I'm bloody and gashed up. "Oh, you didn't get the blueberry pancakes? I'm so sorry. What happened?" It was a great, great moment.

Despite its very offbeat sensibility and its strange mixture of violence and humor, *Pulp Fiction* was a hugely successful movie. For Willis it was perhaps the first time that large audiences really paid attention to his abilities beyond action-hero acrobatics. It gave him hope that it was possible to create a link in Hollywood between art and commerce, between real acting and box-office success.

In 1994, Bruce also appeared in a well-received smaller film, *Nobody's Fool,* based on a novel by Richard Russo and starring Paul Newman, one of Willis's childhood acting heroes. Newman plays a man long estranged from his family who attempts to reacquaint himself with his son and grandson. Willis played a supporting role in the picture, and his performance was highly praised.

Then, in 1995, Bruce found himself in a movie that managed to combine a big Hollywood budget with high-quality writing and a truly interesting role. In Terry Gilliam's scary, funny science fiction thriller *12 Monkeys,* Willis would turn in an incredible performance. Director Gilliam, the highly inventive creator of such offbeat films as *The Fisher King* (1991) and *Time Bandits* (1981), was not afraid that Willis would bring too much "baggage" to the film as a big Hollywood star. As Gilliam later said, "I was impressed by [Willis's] concern to make a good film and not a Bruce Willis vehicle. Also, I like the idea of altering the public's perception of him, so I said, 'Let's do it.' It was potentially dangerous and even disastrous if it had failed. But it didn't."

The movie *12 Monkeys* begins 40 years in the future,

when most of mankind has been wiped out by a mysterious virus and the survivors live underground. Willis plays a prisoner named James Cole, whom scientists choose to send back in time to try to discover what caused the virus in the first place. The assignment is not voluntary. Willis's Cole is, as one writer put it, "[a] man under attack from unknown quarters, very possibly from the very social forces that command him."

Willis portrays Cole as a strong but confused man, haunted by strange, fractured memories and a recurring nightmare, trying hard to make the pieces of a puzzle fall together sensibly. One of the truly great moments in the film, and one of Willis's all-time greatest moments as an actor, is when Cole hears the old song "Blueberry Hill" on the radio, and connects it with his childhood. In an extremely touching moment all the violence, fear, and guardedness fall away from Cole's face as it lights up with the memory of a simpler, happier time in his life.

Still, Bruce did find himself involved with some third-rate blockbusters, such as the action-packed thrillers *The Fifth Element* (1997) and *Armageddon* (1998). In the *Fifth Element,* which takes place in the 23rd century, a cynical Brooklyn cabdriver, played by Willis, unexpectedly becomes involved with an otherworldly woman who can potentially save the earth from an alien attack. The world is also threatened in *Armageddon,* but this time by an approaching asteroid. In the film, which also stars Billy Bob Thornton and Ben Affleck, only Willis and the members of his team can save humanity by destroying the asteroid.

In 1999, Willis outdid himself once again in *The Sixth Sense,* a stylish, haunting thriller about a boy, played by Haley Joel Osment, who claims to see dead people. Willis plays Malcolm Crowe, the child psychologist who wants to help the young boy. One *New York Times* critic described Willis's performance as a triumph of subtlety: "It would have been easy for Mr. Willis to upstage Mr.

Osment, simply by calling attention to his own hurt and showing us the little boy within. He makes a trickier choice: he shows patience and awareness of another actor, a subtle fanning of technique that builds dread—and sympathy for this character."

The 1999 box-office hit The Sixth Sense *received rave reviews. Critics especially acclaimed Bruce's sensitive portrayal of child psychologist Malcom Crowe as he tries to help a disturbed young boy, played by Haley Joel Osment.*

The Sixth Sense went on to earn six Oscar nominations, including Best Picture, and was one of the biggest box-office draws of 1999. But just as audiences a decade earlier seemed to ignore Willis's subtle characterization of a Vietnam vet in the film *In Country,* the panel of Oscar voters overlooked Willis for a Best Actor award. Maybe Willis had distracted them with his campy, smirk-filled, Bruno-ish performance in the comedy *The Whole Nine Yards* (2000), which also starred Matthew Perry, known for his ongoing role in the television series *Friends.* The fact is, although Willis may have already proved his mettle as a serious dramatic actor to his audiences, not everyone sees it yet. But chances are, he'll continue taking risks and working hard until his staunchest critics and skeptics can't help but acknowledge his abilities.

As long as there are writers and directors out there with high-quality projects, the future looks bright for Willis as an actor. But there have been plenty of personal challenges along the way, and there will probably be more. After 11 years together, Willis and Moore announced their intention to divorce in the summer of 1998. Ironically, they had just won a large settlement in a lawsuit against the publishers of a tabloid newspaper for spreading false rumors about their impending breakup. For a year after the announcement they both made themselves virtually invisible, presumably hiding out from the paparazzi somewhere in Idaho. Then, the following summer, they each reemerged while doing publicity work for their new movies.

Although Hollywood's most powerful couple have apparently split for good, it's clear that their decade together was a fruitful, nurturing one on a personal level. From the drunken and dissolute youths they once were, Willis and Moore have emerged as grown-ups. Evidence of this can be found in the very civil, discreet way the two have been behaving in public since their split.

As *People* magazine noted, there have been "no sidewalk screaming matches. No public flings with cute young things. No verbal [missiles] launched by dueling publicists." The November 1998 article suggests that the couple's three daughters play a large role in keeping their parents from behaving in a hostile manner toward each other: "Moore and Willis seem determined to make their split a soft landing for Rumer, 10, Scout, 7, and Tallulah, 4." Soon after their divorce announcement, in fact, Willis and Moore both took their daughters to a Spice Girls concert in Columbus, Ohio, and they later shared parenting duties in Paris while Moore was filming there. They were also together in New Mexico with Moore's terminally ill mother, who died in July 1998 of a brain tumor.

Acquaintances have gone on record to suggest that the

challenges that come with a successful Hollywood career—all that travel and separation—made it impossible for Willis and Moore to live like a normal married couple and remain close. Distance doesn't always make the heart grow fonder. But considering the poor role models each of them had as children, it's commendable that Willis and Moore were able to make their relationship work for as long as it did. With any luck, their intense devotion to the children will allow them to remain friends and to continue to play a positive role in each other's lives and careers.

Like most people, Bruce Willis can behave in contradictory and complicated ways. Although a famous film actor, he seems to want to live a quiet, family-oriented life in rural Idaho, where he guards his privacy closely, with a level of vigilance that some people would call paranoia. At the same time, however, he can occasionally act like a demanding, spoiled superstar in public. Yet Willis is still generally admired for the very thing that was once most difficult for him: speaking his mind in an honest, articulate, and forthright manner.

Bruce's children remain important to him despite his decision to divorce their mother, Demi Moore. Shown here in a 1996 photograph are the two older daughters, Scout (being held) and Rumer Willis.

Bruce Willis, ex-stutterer, used to hate doing interviews. He considered them a gross invasion of his privacy. Despite the worldwide success of *Moonlighting,* Willis waited more than three years before allowing a magazine reporter to interview him. But once he got over his media shyness, he became positively garrulous in the press— ready to talk about anything and everything. Although he has maintained his lifelong (and understandable) hatred of the tabloid media and their extreme disregard for factual accuracy, he has allowed himself to be written about at

In February 2000 Willis showed up at a screening of The Whole Nine Yards *with fellow cast member Rosanna Arquette. The two previously acted together in* Pulp Fiction.

length in more respectable publications such as the *New York Times* and *Esquire* magazine.

In fact, rather than shunning publicity, Willis has become one of those celebrities who mouth off (sometimes amusingly, sometimes annoyingly) on politics, religion, business, relationships, family and children, the movie business, and any sort of topic, no matter how little their expertise may be. In the summer of 1999, as he was doing the required publicity for his new action movie, *Armageddon,* Willis invited a reporter from *George* magazine to visit him at his Hailey ranch. True to form, Willis revealed himself to be a complex combination of "nice guy"—when he offered the reporter a small gift at the door—and "troublemaker"—when he made irreverent, potentially controversial statements about history and politics. For instance, he argued that there's no connection between the violence in some of his movies and the real-life violence that plagues this country. He insisted that, way back in the 1940s, President Franklin D. Roosevelt "knew Pearl Harbor was going to be attacked and let it happen anyway." He called John F. Kennedy a flawed man with "a media team that made him out to be a demigod."

As a culture, we are often fascinated with the opinions of our movie stars, and we especially enjoy it when they say or do things that will get them in trouble or cause a ruckus in the press. If we agree with the troublemaking statement, we get to feel self-righteous when other people criticize the celebrity for saying it. If we disagree with what the celebrity says, we get an uncharitable thrill watching him or her catch heat for it. Movie stars may not have anything particularly interesting or original to say for themselves; in fact, their opinions may often strike us as glib and simpleminded. But we still listen to what film and television celebrities have to say, if only to marvel at the things that come out of their mouths.

Lot of words come out of Bruce Willis's mouth these days, and he doesn't stutter when saying them. He is, like the character David Addison, a man who "plants his feet and speaks his mind." All sorts of words—sensitive, silly, profound, witty, ludicrous, obnoxious—come tumbling out with ease, whether he's acting in front of a movie camera or acting in a more subtle way as "Bruce Willis, superstar," to fulfill the expectations of fans and magazine readers.

From a boy who "could hardly talk," who required "three minutes to complete a sentence," who was crushed by his inability to express himself, Bruce Willis has grown into a rather talkative man—perhaps even a motormouth, in some situations. He is living proof that such transformations are possible, and that weaknesses can indeed be turned into strengths.

CHRONOLOGY

1955 Walter Bruce Willis born to David Willis, an American soldier, and Marlene Willis, a German citizen, on March 19 in Idar-Oberstein, West Germany

1957 After David's discharge from the army, the young family moves back to his home state of New Jersey, settling in Carneys Point

1963 Bruce's stuttering problem begins

1971 David and Marlene Willis divorce

1973 Bruce graduates from Penns Grove High School in Penns Grove, New Jersey

1975 Enrolls at Montclair (N.J.) State College

1977 Leases apartment in the Hell's Kitchen neighborhood of New York City, where he begins his life as "Bruno," the harmonica-playing bartender and struggling actor

1982 Lands a tiny role in *The Verdict,* which stars Paul Newman

1984 Stars in his first major theatrical role, as Eddie in Sam Shepard's play *Fool for Love;* wins his breakthrough role of David Addison in the TV show *Moonlighting*

1986 Breaks up with Sheri Rivera, the first serious girlfriend of his adult life, who had helped him in his career; begins recording his Motown album, *The Return of Bruno,* which eventually sells more than a million copies

1987 Appears in his first leading film role in *Blind Date;* wins the Golden Globe Award for Best Performance by an Actor in a Television Series (Comedy or Musical) and an Emmy for Outstanding Lead Actor in a Drama Series for *Moonlighting;* marries Demi Moore in Las Vegas, Nevada

1988 Appears in *Die Hard,* for which he receives a record-breaking $5 million fee; moves to Hailey, Idaho; Demi and Bruce's first child, daughter Rumer Glenn, is born

1989 Charms audiences with his voice-over role of baby Mikey in *Look Who's Talking;* appears as a troubled, brooding Vietnam vet in *In Country*

1990 Appears in *Die Hard 2: Die Harder*

1991 Appears in the box-office bomb *Hudson Hawk;* second daughter, Scout Larue, is born

1992 Makes a cameo appearance in *The Player;* attempts a new kind of role—a soft-spoken, henpecked nerd—in *Death Becomes Her*

1994   Proves, once again, that he's a capable, serious actor with his multifaceted, riveting performance as a boxer in *Pulp Fiction;* also appears in a supporting role in the acclaimed *Nobody's Fool;* third daughter, Tallulah Belle, is born

1995   Shaves his head to star in Terry Gilliam's science fiction thriller *12 Monkeys;* makes the third and final installment of the *Die Hard* series—*Die Hard with a Vengeance*

1998   Moore and Willis announce plans to divorce

1999   Stars in *The Sixth Sense,* which receives six Oscar nominations, including the nomination for Best Picture

2000   Wins Emmy Award for Outstanding Guest Actor in a Comedy Series for three-episode appearance on *Friends;* stars in a box-office hit *Unbreakable;* announces plans to record a new album

FILMOGRAPHY AND DISCOGRAPHY

SELECTED FILMS AND VIDEOS

The First Deadly Sin (1980)

The Verdict (1982)

Blind Date (1987)

Die Hard (1988)

Sunset (1988)

In Country (1989)

Look Who's Talking, voice (1989)

That's Adequate (1989)

The Bonfire of the Vanities (1990)

Die Hard 2 (1990)

Look Who's Talking Too, voice (1990)

Billy Bathgate (1991)

Hudson Hawk (cowriter) (1991)

The Last Boy Scout (1991)

Mortal Thoughts (1991)

Death Becomes Her (1992)

National Lampoon's Loaded Weapon I, cameo (1992)

The Player, cameo (1992)

Striking Distance (1993)

Nobody's Fool (1994)

Pulp Fiction (1994)

Die Hard with a Vengeance (1995)

Four Rooms (1995)

12 Monkeys (1995)

Last Man Standing (1996)

The Fifth Element (1997)

The Jackal (1997)

Armageddon (1998)

Mercury Rising (1998)

The Siege (1998)

Breakfast of Champions (1999)

The Sixth Sense (1999)

The Story of Us (1999)

The Kid (2000)

Unbreakable (2000)

The Whole Nine Yards (2000)

Bandits (tentative title) (2001)

TELEVISION

1984	*Miami Vice* (guest appearance)
1985–89	*Moonlighting* (series)
1988	*The Return of Bruno* (special; executive producer)
1990	*The Simpsons* (guest voice)
1996	*Bruno the Kid* (animated series; voice; executive producer)
1997	*Mad About You* (guest appearance)
1999	*Ally McBeal* (guest appearance)
2000	*Friends* (three-episode guest appearance)

ALBUMS

| 1987 | *The Return of Bruno* |
| 1989 | *If It Don't Kill You, It Just Makes You Stronger* |

BIBLIOGRAPHY

BOOKS AND ARTICLES

Gerston, Jill. "Finally, Bruce Willis Gets Invited to the Ball." *New York Times,* 2 October 1994.

Gest, Emily. "Demi and Bruce: Life After Love." *Us,* October 1999.

Gliatto, Tom. "Dreams Die Hard." *People Weekly,* 13 July 1998.

Goldberg, Nathaniel. "Bruce Willis Kicks Asteroid." *George,* July 1998.

Grobel, Lawrence. "Playboy Interview: Bruce Willis." *Playboy,* November 1988.

McInerney, Jay. "Bruce Willis in the Hot Zone." *Esquire,* May 1995.

Mitchell, Elvis. "Behind the Deadpan: A Talent Is in Action." *New York Times,* 5 March 2000.

Parker, John. *Bruce Willis: The Unauthorised Biography.* London: Virgin Books, 1997.

Sheff, David. "Playboy Interview: Bruce Willis." *Playboy,* February 1996.

Turan, Kenneth. "Bruce Willis Looks for the Man Within the Icon." *New York Times,* 1 July 1990.

Weinraub, Bernard. "Mr. Misunderstood? Willis Makes Himself Clear." *New York Times,* September 21, 1993.

WEBSITES

E! Online
   http://www. eonline.com

Mr. Showbiz
   http://www.mrshowbiz.go.com

APPENDIX

For Further Information on Stuttering

**Hollins Communication
Research Institute**
P.O. Box 9737
Roanoke, VA 24020
(540) 362-6528
Fax: (540) 362-6663
E-mail: adm-hcri@rbnet.com

National Center for Stuttering
(800) 221-2483;
in New York State call (212) 532-1460

National Stutterers' Hotline
(800) 221-2483 (United States and
Canada)

National Stuttering Project
5100 East La Palma Avenue, Suite 208
Anaheim Hills, CA 92807
(800) 364-1677
Fax: (714) 693-7554
E-mail: nspmail@aol.com

Stuttering Foundation of America
P.O. Box 11749
3100 Walnut Grove Road, #603
Memphis, TN 38111
(800) 992-9392
www.stuttersfa.org
E-mail: stutter@nantek.net

BOOKS AND ARTICLES ABOUT STUTTERING

Brown, Alan, and Grant Forsberg. *Lost Boys Never Say Die.* New York: Delacorte Press,
1989.

Bunting, Eve. *Blackbird Singing.* New York: Macmillan, 1980.

Chambers, Aidan. Seal Secret. New York: Harper and Row, 1980.

Holland, Isabelle. *Alan and the Animal Kingdom.* Philadelphia: Lippincott, 1977.

Stucley, Elizabeth. *The Contrary Orphans.* New York: Franklin Watts, 1961.

Westbrook, J., and J. Ahlbach. *Listen with Your Heart.* Anaheim Hills, CA: National
Stuttering Project, 1996.

Yeoman, Barry. "Wrestling with Words." *Psychology Today,* November/December 1998.

WEBSITE

The Stuttering Home Page, a project of the National Stuttering Association
http://www.mankato.msus.edu/~stutter/

INDEX

PICTURE CREDITS

SANDY ASIRVATHAM is a freelance writer and aspiring musician living in Baltimore, Maryland. She received a bachelor of arts degree in philosophy and economics, and a master of fine arts degree in creative writing, both from Columbia University in New York City. As a very shy child who had trouble speaking her mind, she found herself drawn to acting. Just like the subject of this book, she first learned how to articulate herself while pretending to be someone else onstage. Now, as an adult, she finds it a little too easy to say just about anything to anyone.

JAMES SCOTT BRADY serves on the board of trustees with the Center to Prevent Handgun Violence and is the vice chairman of the Brain Injury Foundation. Mr. Brady served as assistant to the president and White House press secretary under President Ronald Reagan. He was severely injured in an assassination attempt on the president, but remained the White House press secretary until the end of the administration. Since leaving the White House, Mr. Brady has lobbied for stronger gun laws. In November 1993, President Bill Clinton signed the Brady Bill, a national law requiring a waiting period on handgun purchases and a background check on buyers.